For Popcorn Lovers Only

Diane Pfeifer

Illustrations by Clark Taylor

Published by Strawberry Patch, Atlanta, Georgia

Published by: Strawberry Patch
                P.O. Box 52404
                Atlanta, GA 30355

Executive Editor: Marge McDonald
Editor: Susie Blackmun
Cover Photography: Ned Burris
Food Photography: Tricia McCannon
Airbrush: Michael Harless
Stylist: Rhonda Carellas-Voss

Design & Composition: 3x3 Studio, Inc., Atlanta, GA
Printing: Atlanta Graphics, Kingsport, TN

I dedicate this book to my Father
and to world happiness
through the power of popcorn and love.

I would like to thank my mom, Patricia Pfeifer, for craving popcorn instead of pickles before my twin Suzanne and I were born. My deepest thanks to: George Lawes for idea instigating; David Leonard and Micro Music for computer counseling; Nace Few for popcorn posing; Jeff Justice for sampling sweets; Marietta Handy City for bench borrowing; Jay Dishman, Carol O'Connell and Cosby Powell for spiritual support; and Dr. Robert Anthony, whose wonderful words kept me inspired in and out of the kitchen.

A portion of the proceeds of this book will benefit children's charities.

TABLE OF CONTENTS

THE TRUE STORY OF POPCORN

On the first day, God created popcorn.
On the second day, He created man to eat
the popcorn.
On the third day, He created woman to clean
up the mess.
On the fourth day, He created movies and TV
as excuses to eat popcorn.
On the fifth day, He relaxed (with a bowl of
popcorn, of course).
On the sixth and seventh days, He flossed His
teeth.

In the Garden of Eden, life was simple and popcorn
grew on trees. But Adam disobeyed and took a bite
of the forbidden kernel that Eve handed him. They
were banished from the garden and thus began the rise
and fall of popcorn throughout history.

In order to survive through the
ages, Moses established the Ten
Commandments of Popcorn.
They are still followed today
and are listed as a reminder
of correct popcorn behavior.

The Ten Commandments

1.

Thou shalt maketh perfect popcorn by following "Back to Basics."

2.

Thou shalt not causeth harm to animals in pursuit of popcorn passion. However, some animals don't mindeth being milked and laying eggs, so dairy and egg ingredients art included.

3.

Thou shalt cureth any soggy recipe by placing it under thy broiler, but watcheth carefully, as it doth burn faster than a New York minute.

4.

Thou shalt shareth thy popcorn with others, even if the author won't.

5.

Thou shalt findeth certain ingredients in gourmet, coffee and craft shops, once they art invented.

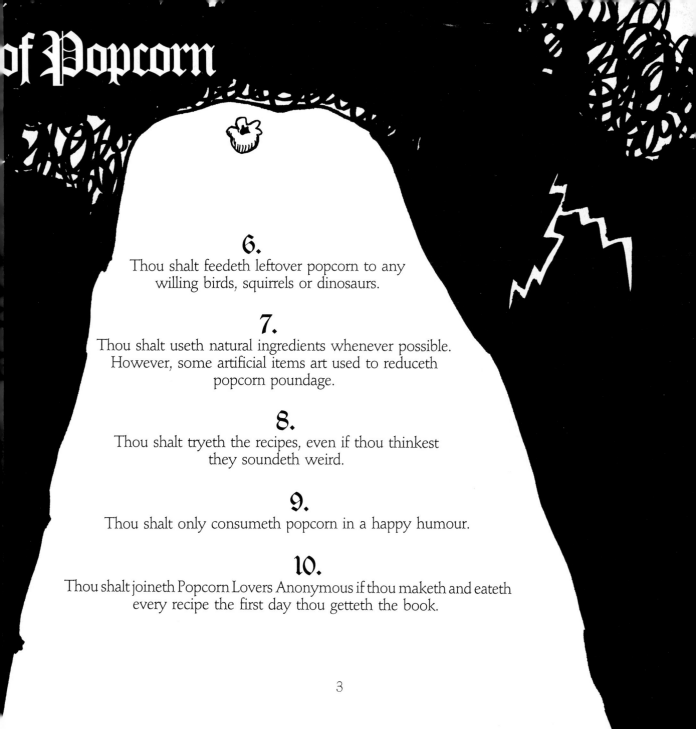

# of Popcorn

6.

Thou shalt feedeth leftover popcorn to any
willing birds, squirrels or dinosaurs.

7.

Thou shalt useth natural ingredients whenever possible.
However, some artificial items art used to reduceth
popcorn poundage.

8.

Thou shalt tryeth the recipes, even if thou thinkest
they soundeth weird.

9.

Thou shalt only consumeth popcorn in a happy humour.

10.

Thou shalt joineth Popcorn Lovers Anonymous if thou maketh and eateth
every recipe the first day thou getteth the book.

BACK TO BASICS

Regular method: ½ cup uncooked popcorn
2 tablespoons cooking oil

1. Heat 3-quart covered saucepan over high heat for 2 minutes.
2. Pour 2 tablespoons cooking oil into pan, covering bottom. Some recipes use different oils for popping.
3. Lower heat to medium high.
4. Add 3 or 4 kernels.
5. When they pop, add rest of popcorn, cover, and shake pan continuously while popcorn is popping.
6. When popping stops, pour into large container. Makes approximately 9-11 cups.

Microwave method: ½ cup uncooked popcorn

Pop popcorn in approved microwave popper according to manufacturer's directions, usually 3-4 minutes on high. If using packaged microwave popcorn, follow package directions.

Low-cal method: ½ cup popcorn

Pop without oil in microwave in approved container or hot air popper according to manufacturer's directions. If using packaged microwave popcorn, check calorie and fat content, as some are high in both.

Calories per cup: 23 (popped without oil)
41 (popped with oil)

POPCORN PONDERINGS
& HELPFUL HINTS

Even though I was a chemist in a previous career, I still turn the page if I see a candy thermometer reading in a recipe. It just looks too complicated and besides, until I wrote this book, I didn't even OWN a thermometer! So I'll explain this and a few other details to make these recipes easy. After all, popcorn is supposed to be fun!

Hard ball stage: When a small amount of boiling mixture dropped into very cold water forms a hard ball. If you insist on taking its temperature, it should reach 250 degrees F.

Hard crack stage: When a small amount of boiling mixture dropped into very cold water forms brittle strands or reaches 300 degrees F, if you must be technical.

While we're on the subject of sweets, you may replace sugar and corn syrup with an equal amount of honey or barley malt, although it may change the taste of the recipe a bit.

For all you calorie cutters, you may replace butter with diet margarine, maple syrup with low-cal syrup, and preserves with low-cal preserves, except when the recipes call for more than ¼ cup. Large amounts contain too much water and believe me, I ended up with some really soggy recipes! (See Third Commandment for the cure in case this ever happens to you). Diet mayonnaise may be substituted for regular, regardless of amount. For you sodium watchers, lite seasonings may be substituted and they cling better as well.

All recipes call for popped popcorn unless otherwise stated. When preparing butter recipes, never let the butter brown while melting. If you like, coat the popcorn in a 14 x 18 x 3-inch greased roasting pan instead of a large bowl. I find it best to toss the mixtures by hand, but let the hot syrup mixtures cool slightly before handling.

When microwaving recipes, always use approved containers. If your microwave oven is low-wattage, you may need to add to the given times. Please use unsalted microwave popcorn, as the salted kind really messes up the recipes.

And, just in case you were wondering, I tested each of these recipes in MY kitchen, so if your pop flops, please don't yell at me. Besides, to a true Popcorn Lover even the messes are good!

POPPING THROUGH
THE AGES

ATTILA THE HUN-EY CRUNCH

6 cups popcorn   ½ cup butter
2 cups Rice Chex cereal   ½ cup honey
2 cups assorted unsalted nuts

Preheat oven to 350 degrees F.

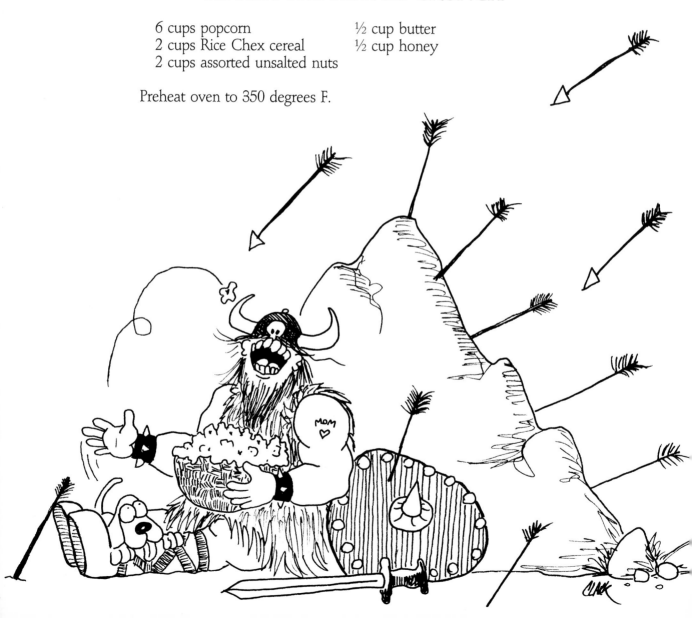

Combine popcorn, cereal and nuts in large greased roasting pan.

Melt butter and honey in small pan over low heat. Stir. Dribble over popcorn. Toss with hands to coat thoroughly.

Bake 10-15 minutes, stirring every 5 minutes.

Worth plundering for.

Microwave method: Combine butter and honey in a 2-quart glass measure. Microwave on high until melted. Continue as above.

Calorie cutter: Decrease cereal to ½ cup. For coating mixture, use ¼ cup diet margarine, ¼ cup honey and ¼ cup diet maple syrup. Nuts are a no-no.

Yield: 10 cups.

ARIS-POP-LE

8 cups popcorn
2 tablespoons butter
1 teaspoon olive oil
⅛ teaspoon garlic powder

¼ cup crumbled feta cheese
3 tablespoons chopped black or
  Greek olives

Place popcorn in large bowl.

Melt butter in small pan over low heat. Remove from heat. Stir in olive oil and garlic powder.

Dribble over popcorn. Toss with hands to coat thoroughly.

Squeeze feta cheese in paper towel to remove excess moisture. Crumble. Toss cheese and olives into popcorn.

Beware of gifts bearing Greek popcorn!

Calorie cutter: Use diet margarine and 1 tablespoon feta cheese. Omit olive oil or use low-cal vegetable oil.

Yield: About 8 cups.

JULIUS CAESAR SALAD CORN

8 cups popcorn
1 tablespoon butter

1 tablespoon olive oil
1 tablespoon lemon juice
½ teaspoon coarsely ground
  black pepper
1 tablespoon powdered egg
  substitute
2 tablespoons grated
  Parmesan cheese

Place popcorn in large bowl.

Melt butter in small pan over low heat. Remove from heat. Stir in olive oil, lemon juice, pepper and egg mix.

Dribble over popcorn. Toss with hands to coat thoroughly. Sprinkle with Parmesan cheese.

I'm having some – "Et tu, Bruté?"

Calorie cutter: Use 2 tablespoons diet margarine. Omit olive oil.

Shortcut: To make coating mixture, combine 1 tablespoon dry Caesar salad dressing with melted butter and oil.

Yield: 8 cups.

CONFUCIUS CORN

8 cups popcorn
1 cup chow mein noodles
1 tablespoon butter

1 tablespoon soy sauce or tamari
¼ teaspoon garlic powder
⅛ teaspoon ginger powder

Place popcorn and noodles in large bowl.

Melt butter in small pan over low heat. Remove from heat. Stir in remaining ingredients.

Dribble over popcorn. Toss with hands to coat thoroughly.

Make two batches, as you'll be hungry again in an hour.

Yield: 9 cups.

MARC ANTONY NIBBLE

8 cups popcorn
1 7-ounce jar marshmallow
cream

¾ cup peanut butter
2 tablespoons butter
½ cup peanuts (optional)

Place popcorn in large bowl.

Combine marshmallow cream, peanut butter and butter in large sauce-pan over low heat. Stir until smooth. Remove from heat.

Pour over popcorn and stir to coat thoroughly. Toss in peanuts if desired.

Be sure this recipe doesn't nibble you!

Variations: If you like yours chewy, place popcorn mixture on baking sheet lined with wax paper. Freeze for 1 hour. Serve cold.

Yield: 8 cups.

CLEO-POP-RA

8 cups popcorn
2 tablespoons flaked coconut
2 tablespoons butter
¼ teaspoon onion powder
¼ teaspoon garlic powder

¼ teaspoon nutmeg
¼ teaspoon parsley flakes
¼ teaspoon lite lemon pepper
⅛ teaspoon coriander
Dash cayenne pepper

Combine popcorn and coconut in large bowl.

Melt butter in small pan over low heat. Remove from heat. Stir in remaining ingredients.

Dribble over popcorn mixture. Toss with hands to coat thoroughly.

Check for rattling noises before eating.

Yield: 8 cups.

JOAN OF ARC CAMPFIRE CORN

8 cups popcorn
2 tablespoons butter

1 7-ounce jar marshmallow
  cream

Preheat oven to 350 degrees F.

Place popcorn in large greased bowl.

Melt butter in saucepan over low heat. Stir in marshmallow cream until smooth. Remove from heat.

Pour over popcorn and stir to coat thoroughly.

Spread popcorn mixture on greased baking sheet. Bake for 10 minutes. Or, for a crunchier effect, place under broiler for 1 minute. Stir occasionally to be sure popcorn is not burning.

Remove·and cool before serving.

You won't feel like a martyr eating this!

Microwave method: Place butter in 3-quart glass casserole. Microwave on high until melted. Stir in marshmallow cream. Cook 1 minute on medium high. Continue as above.

Yield: 8 cups.

17

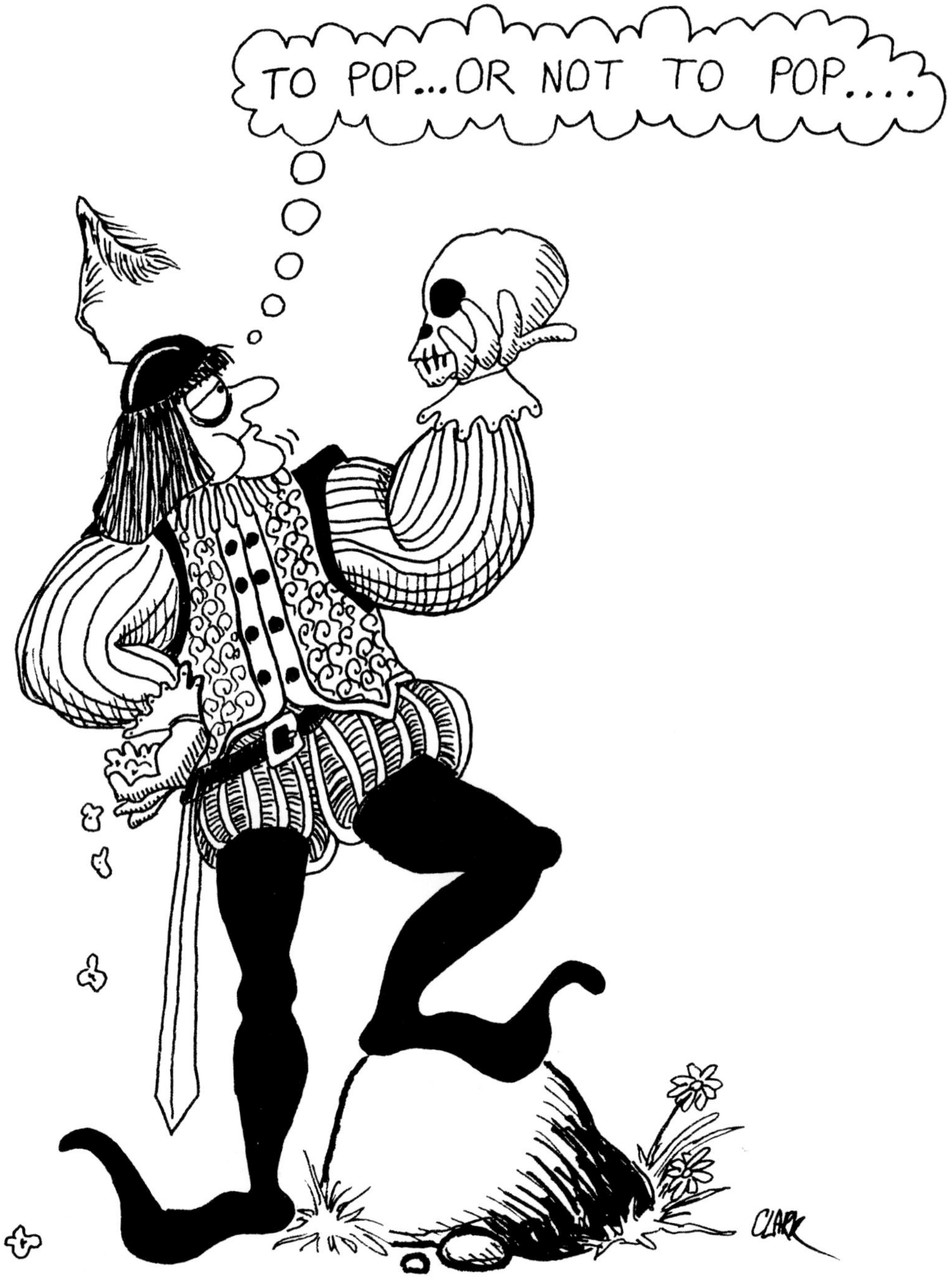
TO POP...OR NOT TO POP....
CLARK

HAMLET DANISH CRUMB CRUNCH

8 cups popcorn
⅓ cup firmly packed brown
  sugar
¼ cup flour

¼ teaspoon baking powder
5 tablespoons softened butter
Powdered sugar

Place popcorn in large bowl.

Mix sugar, flour and baking powder. With a fork, cut in 2½ tablespoons butter until pea-sized crumbs form.

Spread on baking sheet. Place under broiler for 1 minute. Stir. Check constantly to be sure mixture is not burning. Remove and cool before serving.

Melt remaining butter and dribble over popcorn. Toss with hands to coat thoroughly. Mix in crumbs and dust with powdered sugar.

Perfect for those times you feel like a crumb!

Calorie cutter: Add half the crumb mixture to popcorn. Don't re-coat with extra butter. Dust with 1 packet sweetener.

Yield: 8 cups.

MONA LISA PIZZA CORN

½ cup unpopped popcorn
2 tablespoons olive oil
1 tablespoon cooking oil
2 tablespoons butter
1 tablespoon tomato paste
½ teaspoon oregano
¼ teaspoon basil
¼ teaspoon thyme
¼ teaspoon paprika
¼ teaspoon garlic powder
¼ teaspoon onion powder
2 tablespoons grated Parmesan
  cheese
1 cup shredded mozzarella
  cheese

Pop popcorn with 1 tablespoon olive oil and 1 tablespoon cooking oil. Set aside in large bowl.

Melt butter and remaining olive oil in small pan over low heat. Remove from heat.

Stir in tomato paste, spices and Parmesan cheese. Dribble over popcorn. Toss with hands to coat thoroughly.

Spread popcorn mixture on greased baking sheet and sprinkle with mozzarella. Place under broiler for 1 minute or until cheese melts. Check constantly to be sure popcorn is not burning.

Eat it warm or pretend it was delivered and eat it cold.

Calorie cutter: Pop popcorn without oil.* Use 2 tablespoons diet margarine, omit olive oil and reduce mozzarella to ¼ cup.

Shortcut: Substitute 4 teaspoons dry spaghetti sauce mix and 2 teaspoons water for tomato paste and spices.

Variations: Add favorite pizza toppings before broiling – chopped fresh green peppers, finely chopped black olives, diced mushrooms, soy bacon bits or other toppings.

Yield: About 10 cups.

*See page 6.

DA VINCI PESTO POP

8 cups popcorn
3 tablespoons butter
1 teaspoon dried basil

½ teaspoon garlic powder
½ cup grated Parmesan cheese
½ cup toasted pine nuts

Place popcorn in large bowl.

Melt butter in small pan over low heat. Remove from heat. Stir in basil and garlic powder.

Dribble over popcorn. Toss with hands to coat thoroughly. Sprinkle with Parmesan cheese and toss in toasted pine nuts.

Presto – pesto!

Calorie cutter: Use diet margarine, ¼ cup Parmesan cheese and 2 tablespoons pine nuts.

Shortcut: Make coating mixture with 2 tablespoons dry pesto sauce mix and butter.

Yield: 8 cups.

NAPOLEON BONA-POP

8 cups popcorn
1 tablespoon butter
2 teaspoons lemon juice
1 tablespoon powdered egg
  substitute

½ teaspoon tarragon
½ teaspoon lite lemon pepper
Dash cayenne pepper
1 teaspoon dried chives
Salt to taste

Place popcorn in large bowl.

Melt butter in small pan over low heat. Remove from heat and stir in remaining ingredients.

Spoon over popcorn. Toss with hands to coat thoroughly.

Voilá!

Shortcut: Make coating mixture with 1 tablespoon dry Bernaise sauce mix and 2 tablespoons butter.

Yield: 8 cups.

CHRISTOPHER COLUMBUS CORN

8 cups popcorn
2 tablespoons butter
1 teaspoon olive oil
¼ teaspoon oregano
¼ teaspoon basil

⅛ teaspoon marjoram
⅛ teaspoon garlic powder
⅛ teaspoon onion powder
2 tablespoons grated Parmesan
  cheese

Place popcorn in large bowl.

Melt butter and oil in small pan over low heat. Remove from heat. Stir in oregano, basil, marjoram, garlic powder and onion powder.

Dribble over popcorn. Toss with hands to coat thoroughly. Sprinkle with Parmesan cheese.

Share your discovery with friends.

Yield: 8 cups.

VAN GOGH DUTCH APPLEPOP

8 cups popcorn
1 tablespoon butter
1 tablespoon frozen apple juice
  concentrate, thawed
¼ teaspoon cinnamon

⅛ teaspoon allspice
1 teaspoon brown sugar
½ cup diced dried apples
½ cup raisins
½ cup chopped walnuts

Place popcorn in large bowl.

Melt butter in small pan over low heat. Remove from heat. Stir in juice, cinnamon, allspice and brown sugar.

Dribble over popcorn. Toss with hands to coat thoroughly. Mix in apples, raisins and nuts. Sprinkle with extra brown sugar, and cinnamon if desired.

You'd cut off an ear for this, too – corn, that is.

Variations: Use 1 tablespoon applesauce or apple jelly instead of juice.

Yield: About 9 cups.

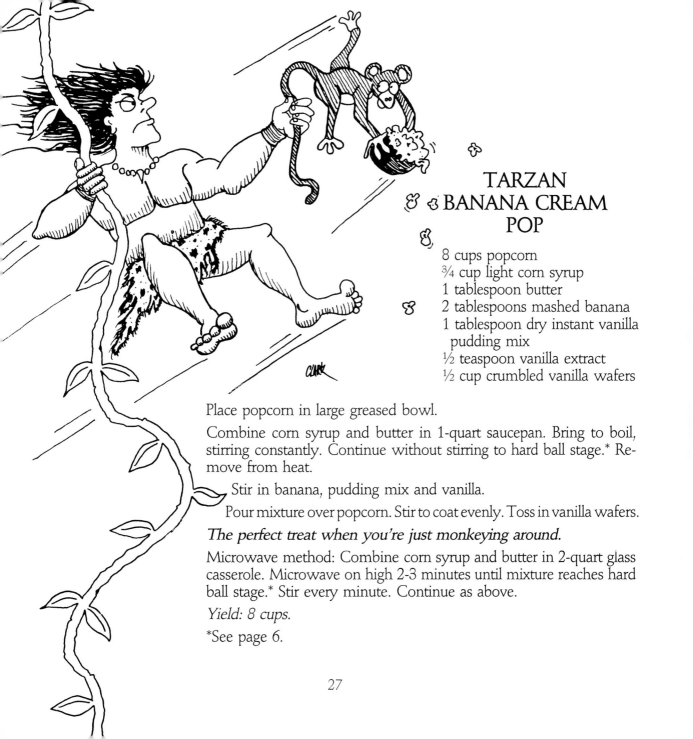

TARZAN & BANANA CREAM POP

8 cups popcorn
¾ cup light corn syrup
1 tablespoon butter
2 tablespoons mashed banana
1 tablespoon dry instant vanilla
  pudding mix
½ teaspoon vanilla extract
½ cup crumbled vanilla wafers

Place popcorn in large greased bowl.

Combine corn syrup and butter in 1-quart saucepan. Bring to boil, stirring constantly. Continue without stirring to hard ball stage.* Remove from heat.

Stir in banana, pudding mix and vanilla.

Pour mixture over popcorn. Stir to coat evenly. Toss in vanilla wafers.

The perfect treat when you're just monkeying around.

Microwave method: Combine corn syrup and butter in 2-quart glass casserole. Microwave on high 2-3 minutes until mixture reaches hard ball stage.* Stir every minute. Continue as above.

Yield: 8 cups.

*See page 6.

THE GODPOPPER

½ cup uncooked popcorn
3 tablespoons olive oil
1 tablespoon butter

3 cloves fresh garlic, pressed
3 tablespoons grated Parmesan
  cheese

Pop popcorn using 2 tablespoons olive oil instead of cooking oil. Set aside in large bowl.

Melt butter in small pan over low heat. Stir in remaining olive oil. Add garlic to pan and sauté briefly.

Dribble over popcorn. Toss with hands to coat thoroughly. Sprinkle with Parmesan cheese.

Serve – or else!

Calorie cutter: Pop popcorn without oil.* Sauté garlic in 2 tablespoons diet margarine and add 2 tablespoons Parmesan cheese.

Shortcut: Substitute 1 tablespoon bottled garlic butter and 1 tablespoon butter for coating mixture.

Variations: For a crunchier effect, spread popcorn mixture on greased baking sheet and place under broiler for 1 minute. Check constantly to be sure popcorn is not burning. Remove and cool before serving.

Yield: 8 cups.

*See page 6.

POPCORN AROUND THE WORLD

31

IRISH COFFEE CRUNCH

8 cups popcorn
¾ cup light corn syrup
2 tablespoons butter
1 teaspoon instant coffee
1 tablespoon non-dairy
  creamer

1 teaspoon vanilla extract
½ teaspoon rum or brandy
  extract

Place popcorn in large greased bowl.

Combine remaining ingredients in 1-quart saucepan. Bring to boil, stirring constantly. Continue without stirring to hard ball stage.*

Pour over popcorn. Stir to coat evenly. Cool and serve.

Invite a leprechaun over.

Microwave method: Combine corn syrup, butter, coffee, creamer and extracts in 2-quart glass casserole. Microwave on high 2-3 minutes until mixture reaches hard ball stage.* Stir every minute. Continue as above.

Yield: 8 cups.

*See page 6.

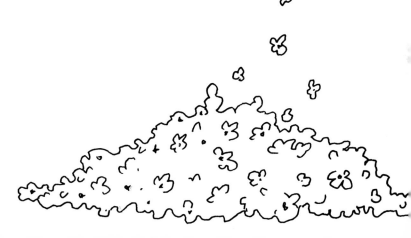

BUTTER "SCOTCH" BARS

8 cups popcorn
1 cup granola
1 6-ounce package
  butterscotch chips
⅓ cup peanut butter

2 tablespoons butter
⅛ teaspoon salt
1 7-ounce jar marshmallow
  cream

Combine popcorn and granola in a greased 9 x 13 x 2-inch baking pan.

Melt butterscotch chips, peanut butter, butter and salt in large saucepan over low heat. Stir until smooth. Remove from heat. Stir in marshmallow cream. Pour over popcorn mixture. Stir to coat evenly.

Press mixture firmly in pan. Refrigerate until set, about 4 hours. Cut into bars and serve.

Be thrifty – save one bar for tomorrow.

Microwave method: Combine butterscotch chips, peanut butter, butter and salt in 3-quart glass casserole. Microwave on medium high until melted. Stir every minute. Remove. Continue as above.

Yield: About 18 bars.

33

34

FRENCH ONION MELT

8 cups popcorn
2 tablespoons butter
1 tablespoon dry onion
   bouillon
1 tablespoon minced onion

3 tablespoons shredded
   mozzarella cheese
1 cup canned French-fried
   onions

Place popcorn in large bowl.

Melt butter in small pan over low heat. Remove from heat. Stir in bouillon and onion.

Dribble over popcorn. Toss with hands to coat thoroughly.

Spread popcorn mixture on greased baking sheet. Sprinkle with cheese and place under broiler 1 minute. Check constantly to be sure popcorn is not burning. Remove and cool. Toss in French-fried onions. Serve.

Magnifique!

Calorie cutter: Use lowfat mozzarella cheese and forget the French-fried onions.

Shortcut: Substitute 1 tablespoon dry onion soup mix for bouillon and onion.

Yield: 8 cups.

GERMAN BEER BARREL MIX

½ cup butter
4 slices pumpernickel bread,
  toasted
8 cups popcorn
2 cups pretzel sticks
  or twists

1 tablespoon brown
  mustard
1 teaspoon caraway seeds,
  crushed
½ teaspoon dried dillweed

Butter toast evenly. Cut into ½-inch cubes. Combine bread cubes, popcorn and pretzels in large bowl.

Melt 3 tablespoons butter in small pan over low heat. Remove from heat. Stir in mustard, caraway seeds and dillweed.

Dribble over popcorn mixture. Toss with hands to coat thoroughly.

Have a barrel of fun!

Calorie cutter: Use diet margarine. Use 2 slices unbuttered low-cal wheat bread. Decrease pretzels to ½ cup.

Yield: About 10-12 cups.

AFRICAN JUNGLE CRUNCH

8 cups popcorn
½ cup honey
½ cup butter

1 teaspoon cinnamon
1 small box animal crackers

Preheat oven to 300 degrees F.

Place popcorn in large greased roasting pan.

Melt honey, butter and cinnamon in small pan over low heat.

Dribble over popcorn. Stir to coat thoroughly. Bake 10-15 minutes, stirring every 5 minutes. Remove from oven. Place in large bowl and cool. Toss in animal crackers.

Even vegetarians like this one!

Microwave method: Place honey, butter and cinnamon in 2-cup glass measure. Microwave on high until melted. Continue as above.

Calorie cutter: Substitute ¼ cup diet margarine, ¼ cup honey and ¼ cup diet maple syrup for honey-butter mixture.

Yield: 9 cups.

DUTCH CHOCOLATE POPBALLS

8 cups popcorn
1 tablespoon butter
¼ cup light corn syrup

¾ cup sugar
¼ teaspoon vanilla extract
1 cup chocolate chips

Place popcorn in large greased bowl.

Combine remaining ingredients in small saucepan over medium heat. Cook until chocolate is melted and sugar dissolved, stirring frequently. Continue without stirring until mixture reaches hard ball stage.*

Pour over popcorn. Stir to coat evenly. Cool slightly.

Grease hands and shape mixture into balls, using about ½ cupful for each. Place on baking sheet lined with wax paper and freeze for 1 hour before serving.

A real Dutch treat!

Microwave method: Combine all ingredients except popcorn in 2-quart glass casserole. Microwave on high 2-3 minutes until mixture reaches hard ball stage.* Continue as above.

Calorie cutter: Use sugar-free chocolate.

Variations: Substitute carob chips for chocolate.

Yield: 14-16 popcorn balls.

*See page 6.

MEXI-CORN

8 cups popcorn
1 tablespoon butter
½ cup shredded Monterey
  jack cheese

1 tablespoon chopped jalapeño
  peppers

Place popcorn in large bowl.

Melt butter in small pan over low heat. Add cheese and peppers, stirring until cheese is slightly melted.

Dribble over popcorn. Stir to coat evenly, and serve.

For a crunchier effect, spread popcorn mixture on greased baking sheet and place under broiler for 1 minute. Check constantly to be sure popcorn is not burning. Remove and cool before serving. Add more peppers, if desired.

Some like it hot!

Microwave method: Combine butter, cheese and peppers in 2-cup glass measure. Microwave on high until melted. Continue as above.

Calorie cutter: Use ¼ cup lowfat cheese.

Shortcut: Substitute ½ cup hot pepper cheese for cheese and peppers.

Yield: 8 cups.

RUSSIAN STROGA-POP

8 cups popcorn
1 tablespoon butter
1 tablespoon plain yogurt

¼ teaspoon liquid or dry smoke seasoning
¼ teaspoon soy sauce or tamari

Place popcorn in large bowl.

Melt butter in small pan over low heat. Remove from heat. Stir in yogurt, smoke seasoning and soy sauce.

Dribble over popcorn. Toss with hands to coat thoroughly.

Spread popcorn mixture on greased baking sheet. Place under broiler for 1 minute. Check constantly to be sure popcorn is not burning. Remove and cool before serving.

Worth defecting for!

Calorie cutter: Use lowfat yogurt.

Yield: 8 cups.

POPCORNO PARMESANO, ITALIANO

8 cups popcorn
¼ cup butter
¼ teaspoon garlic powder

½ cup grated Parmesan cheese

Place popcorn in large bowl.

Melt butter in small pan over low heat. Remove from heat. Stir in garlic powder and ¼ cup Parmesan cheese.

Dribble over popcorn. Toss thoroughly to coat. Sprinkle with remaining cheese and toss again.

Ciao down!

Calorie cutter: Use 2 tablespoons each diet margarine and Parmesan cheese.

Yield: 8 cups.

SPANISH OMELET

8 cups popcorn
1 tablespoon butter
2 teaspoons tomato paste
  or dry tomato soup mix
2 tablespoons powdered
  egg mix

1 tablespoon dried green
  pepper flakes
1 tablespoon minced onion
¼ teaspoon black pepper
Dash cayenne pepper
Salt to taste

Place popcorn in large bowl.

Melt butter in small pan over low heat. Remove from heat. Stir in tomato paste or soup mix. Mixture will be quite thick. Stir in remaining ingredients.

Spoon onto popcorn. Toss with hands to coat thoroughly.

For a crunchier effect, spread popcorn mixture on greased baking sheet. Place under broiler 1 minute. Check constantly to be sure popcorn is not burning. Remove and cool before serving.

It's safe to eat – no bull!

Variations: Add soy bacon bits.

Yield: 8 cups popcorn.

43

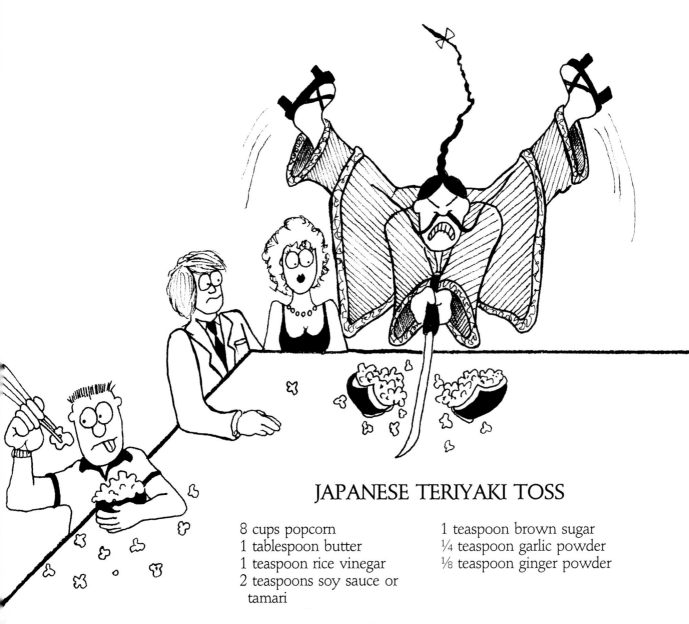

JAPANESE TERIYAKI TOSS

8 cups popcorn
1 tablespoon butter
1 teaspoon rice vinegar
2 teaspoons soy sauce or
  tamari

1 teaspoon brown sugar
¼ teaspoon garlic powder
⅛ teaspoon ginger powder

Place popcorn in large bowl.

Melt butter in small pan over low heat. Remove from heat. Stir in remaining ingredients.

Dribble over popcorn. Toss with hands to coat thoroughly.

Leave shoes outside, please!

Shortcut: Melt butter with 1 tablespoon dry or liquid teriyaki sauce in place of all other ingredients.

Yield: 8 cups.

SZECHUAN STIR-FRY

8 cups popcorn
2 tablespoons sesame oil
4 tablespoons peanut butter, or
2 tablespoons each sesame paste
  and peanut butter
2 tablespoons soy sauce or
  tamari

1 teaspoon garlic powder
¼ teaspoon ginger powder
¼ teaspoon cayenne pepper or
  chili oil to taste
2 teaspoons brown or powdered
  sugar
2 teaspoons rice vinegar

Set popcorn aside in large bowl.

Combine remaining ingredients in large measuring cup.

Preheat wok on warm or place large skillet over low heat for 1 minute.

Add sesame mixture and stir. Quickly add popcorn, stir-frying with large wooden spoons until pieces are evenly coated. Remove from heat. Serve while warm or store in refrigerator in covered container.

So good, you'll wok a mile for it!

Microwave method: Place all ingredients except popcorn in 2-cup glass measure. Microwave 1 minute on medium high. Stir to blend. Dribble over popcorn. Toss with hands to coat thoroughly.

Variations: Add ½ cup unsalted peanuts to popcorn mixture before heating.

Yield: 8 cups.

CHINESE SWEET 'N SOUR

8 cups popcorn
2 tablespoons light corn syrup
½ teaspoon soy sauce
1 tablespoon rice vinegar
1 tablespoon tomato paste or
  dry tomato soup mix
¼ teaspoon onion powder
¼ teaspoon garlic powder
2 tablespoons dried green
  pepper
1 tablespoon diced dried
  pineapple
Salt to taste

Place popcorn in large bowl.

Mix remaining ingredients in large measuring cup. Dribble over popcorn. Toss with hands to coat thoroughly.

Serve with chopsticks and keep a vacuum handy.

Calorie cutter: Use diet maple syrup instead of corn syrup.

Shortcut: Substitute 2 tablespoons liquid sweet 'n sour sauce for coating mixture.

Yield: 8 cups.

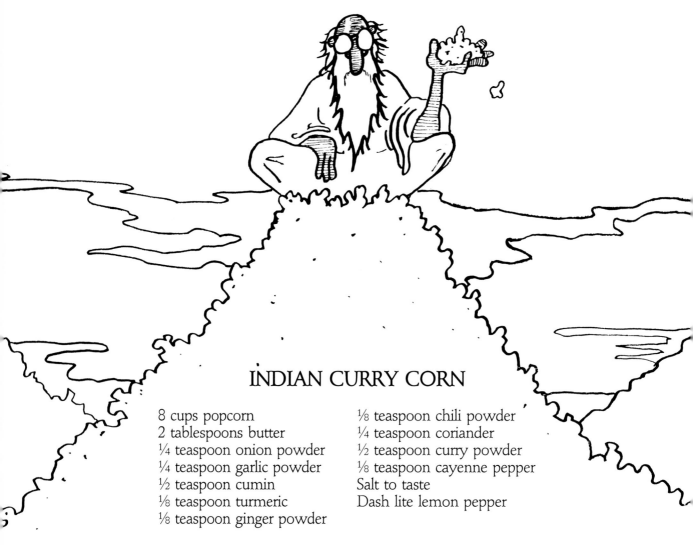

INDIAN CURRY CORN

8 cups popcorn
2 tablespoons butter
¼ teaspoon onion powder
¼ teaspoon garlic powder
½ teaspoon cumin
⅛ teaspoon turmeric
⅛ teaspoon ginger powder

⅛ teaspoon chili powder
¼ teaspoon coriander
½ teaspoon curry powder
⅛ teaspoon cayenne pepper
Salt to taste
Dash lite lemon pepper

Place popcorn in large bowl.

Melt butter in small pan over low heat. Remove from heat. Stir in remaining ingredients.

Dribble over popcorn. Toss with hands to coat thoroughly.

Serve and watch "Gandhi" (it may take more batches).

Shortcut: Make coating mixture with butter and 1 tablespoon prepared curry powder (how unadventurous).

Variations: Add raisins, flaked coconut, dates, dried apples, almonds, or other unsalted nuts.

Yield: 8 cups.

SWISS MOCHA ALMOND

8 cups popcorn	¼ teaspoon instant coffee
1 cup toasted almonds	½ teaspoon vanilla extract
12 ounces Swiss chocolate bars	½ teaspoon almond extract
1 tablespoon butter	1 tablespoon powdered sugar

Combine popcorn and almonds in large greased bowl.

Melt chocolate and butter in small pan over low heat, stirring until smooth. Remove from heat.

Dissolve coffee in extracts and stir into chocolate mixture.

Dribble over popcorn mixture. Stir to coat evenly. Dust with powdered sugar. Spread on baking sheet lined with wax paper. Freeze for 1 hour.

A little treat for your next skiing trip in the Alps.

Microwave method: Combine chocolate and butter in 2-quart glass casserole. Microwave on medium high until melted. Stir every minute. Continue as above.

Calorie cutter: Use 2 tablespoons diet margarine, 1 packet sugar-free cocoa and 2 packets sweetener in place of chocolate bars and butter. Reduce coffee to ⅛ teaspoon. Use ¼ cup almonds or delete altogether.

Variations: Substitute carob bars for chocolate.

Yield: 9 cups.

PARTY POPCORN

PARTY MIX POP

6 cups popcorn	¼ teaspoon garlic powder
4 cups any Chex cereal	1 teaspoon lite seasoning
1 cup unsalted nuts	salt
½ cup butter	⅛ teaspoon cayenne pepper
5 teaspoons Worcestershire sauce	

Preheat oven to 250 degrees F.

Place popcorn, cereal and nuts in large roasting pan.

Melt butter in small pan over low heat. Remove from heat. Stir in Worcestershire sauce, garlic powder, seasoning salt and cayenne.

Pour over popcorn mixture. Toss with hands to coat thoroughly. Bake 45 minutes, stirring every 15 minutes. Remove and serve.

Great excuse for having a party!

Microwave method: Place butter in 6-quart glass casserole. Microwave on high until melted. Stir in remaining ingredients, adding popcorn last. Microwave on high until crisp, 2-3 minutes. Stir every minute.

Calorie cutter: Use ¼ cup diet margarine. No nuts – in the recipe, that is, not at the party!

Variations: Try different cereals and nuts. Add pretzels, corn chips or other snacks to final mixture.

Yield: About 11 cups.

BACORN HORSERADISH

8 cups popcorn
1 tablespoon butter
1 tablespoon mayonnaise
1 tablespoon smooth cottage
  cheese or plain yogurt

1 teaspoon prepared
  horseradish
2 tablespoons soy bacon
  bits

Place popcorn in large bowl.

Melt butter in small pan over low heat. Remove from heat. Stir in mayonnaise, cottage cheese or yogurt, horseradish and soy bacon bits.

Dribble over popcorn. Toss with hands to coat thoroughly. Sprinkle with extra bacon bits, if desired.

Better yet, just keep the popcorn plain and use the mixture like a dip. (No, I didn't mean YOU!)

Yield: 8 cups.

RANCH DRESSING DREAM

8 cups popcorn
1½ tablespoons mayonnaise

2 teaspoons dry ranch
  dressing mix

Place popcorn in large bowl.

Spoon mayonnaise onto popcorn. Toss with hands to coat thoroughly.

Sprinkle with dressing mix and toss again.

This ranch is more fun than Southfork!

Shortcut: Use 1½ tablespoons bottled ranch dressing.

Yield: 8 cups.

SOUR CREAM 'N CHIVES

8 cups popcorn
2 tablespoons butter
1 tablespoon smooth cottage
  cheese or plain yogurt
¼ teaspoon garlic powder

¼ teaspoon onion powder
2 tablespoons dried chives
2 cups sour cream 'n chive
  potato chips, crumbled

Place popcorn in large bowl.

Melt butter in small pan over low heat. Remove from heat and stir in cottage cheese or yogurt, garlic powder, onion powder and chives.

Dribble over popcorn. Toss with hands to coat thoroughly. Spread popcorn mixture on greased baking sheet and place under broiler for 1 minute. Check constantly to be sure popcorn is not burning. Remove and cool. Toss in potato chips and extra chives.

It's terrific – no chive!

Yield: 10 cups.

DAIQUIRI FREEZE

8 cups popcorn
2 tablespoons frozen limeade
  concentrate, thawed
2 tablespoons vanilla
  pudding mix

1 tablespoon powdered
  sugar
¼ teaspoon rum extract

Place popcorn in large casserole.

Combine remaining ingredients.

Dribble over popcorn. Toss with hands to coat thoroughly. If mixture is too tart, dust with extra powdered sugar.

Cover and freeze for 1 hour.

Serve on the nearest beach.

Calorie cutter: Use 2 tablespoons fresh lime juice and dust with 1-2 packets sweetener in place of concentrate and sugar. Stick with regular pudding, as sugar-free type has an aftertaste.

Variations: Add ½ teaspoon banana or strawberry extract for flavored daiquiri effect.

Yield: 8 cups.

KAHLUA KORN

8 cups popcorn
¾ cup light corn syrup
2 tablespoons butter
1 teaspoon instant coffee
  powder

1 teaspoon vanilla extract
½ teaspoon rum extract

Place popcorn in large greased bowl.

Combine remaining ingredients in 1-quart saucepan over low heat. Bring to boil, stirring constantly. Continue without stirring to hard ball stage.*

Pour over popcorn. Stir to coat evenly.

Spread popcorn mixture on greased baking sheet. Place under broiler for 1 minute. Check constantly to be sure popcorn is not burning. Remove and cool before serving.

The perfect after-dinner treat for coffee achievers.

Microwave method: Combine corn syrup, butter, coffee and extracts in 2-quart glass casserole. Microwave on high 2-3 minutes until mixture reaches hard ball stage.* Stir every minute. Continue as above.

Yield: 8 cups.

*See page 6.

PIÑA COLADA COOLER

8 cups popcorn
½ cup dried pineapple, diced
¾ cup flaked coconut
1 tablespoon pineapple juice

1 teaspoon coconut extract
¼ teaspoon pineapple extract
¼ teaspoon rum extract
1 tablespoon powdered sugar

Place popcorn and pineapple in large bowl.

Soak coconut in pineapple juice for a few minutes. Stir in extracts.

Dribble over popcorn. Toss with hands to coat thoroughly. Dust with powdered sugar and serve.

Watch "Hawaii Five-O" and dream on.

Calorie cutter: Use ½ cup coconut and dust with 1-2 packets sweetener in place of sugar.

Shortcut: Use 2 tablespoons piña colada concentrate in place of pineapple juice and extracts.

Yield: 8 cups.

PEANUT BUTTER POP CUPS

8 cups popcorn
1 cup unsalted peanuts
½ cup peanut butter

½ cup chocolate chips
1 tablespoon butter

Place popcorn and peanuts in large greased bowl.

Melt peanut butter, chocolate chips and butter in small pan over low heat, stirring until blended.

Dribble over popcorn and nuts. Stir to coat evenly. Press ½-cup portions into muffin tins lined with foil muffin papers.

Freeze until firm, about 1 hour.

E.T.'s favorite.

Microwave method: Place peanut butter, chocolate chips and butter in 3-quart glass casserole. Microwave on high until melted. Stir every minute. Continue as above.

Calorie cutter: Melt 1 tablespoon diet margarine, 1 packet sugar-free cocoa, 2 packets sweetener and 1 tablespoon peanut butter. Stir. You weren't thinking about adding peanuts, were you?

Shortcut: Melt 10 regular-sized peanut butter cups with 1 tablespoon butter for coating mixture.

Yield: 14-16 muffins.

EL TACO CORNO

8 cups popcorn
1 cup crumbled tortilla
 or corn chips
2 tablespoons butter
¼ teaspoon cumin
¼ teaspoon oregano
⅛ teaspoon garlic powder

¼ teaspoon chili powder
⅛ teaspoon onion powder
¼ teaspoon cayenne pepper
 or to taste
1 tablespoon minced onion
½ cup grated cheddar cheese

Combine popcorn and chips in large bowl.

Melt butter in small pan over low heat. Remove from heat. Stir in remaining ingredients, except cheese.

Dribble over popcorn. Toss with hands to coat thoroughly.

Spread on greased baking sheet and sprinkle with cheese. Place under broiler until cheese melts, about 1 minute. Check constantly to be sure popcorn is not burning. Remove and cool before serving.

Olé!

Calorie cutter: Use diet margarine and ¼ cup lowfat cheese.

Shortcut: Substitute 1 teaspoon taco mix for spices.

Yield: 9 cups.

NACHO MELT

8 cups popcorn
1 cup crumbled tortilla
  chips
2 tablespoons non-lard
  bean dip
¼ teaspoon cumin
¼ teaspoon oregano

¼ teaspoon chili powder
⅛ teaspoon garlic powder
⅛ teaspoon onion powder
⅛ teaspoon cayenne pepper
  or to taste
½ cup grated cheddar or
  Monterey jack cheese

Combine popcorn and chips in large bowl.

Place bean dip in small bowl. Stir in remaining ingredients, except cheese.

Spoon onto popcorn. Toss with hands to coat thoroughly.

Spread popcorn mixture on greased baking sheet. Sprinkle with cheese and place under broiler until cheese melts, about 1 minute. Check constantly to be sure popcorn is not burning. Remove and cool before serving.

Just what you've bean hungry for!

Calorie cutter: Use 2 tablespoons lowfat cheese.

Variations: Top with chopped jalapeño peppers before broiling.

Yield: 9 cups.

SESAME SURPRISE

8 cups popcorn
1 tablespoon tahini
 (sesame paste)
1 tablespoon butter
2 teaspoons soy sauce
 or tamari

1 teaspoon lemon juice
1 teaspoon sesame oil
¼ teaspoon garlic powder
⅛ teaspoon cayenne pepper
2 tablespoons sesame seeds,
 toasted

Place popcorn in large bowl.

Melt tahini and butter in small pan over low heat with soy sauce, lemon juice, sesame oil, garlic powder and cayenne. Remove from heat. Stir until smooth.

Dribble over popcorn. Toss with hands to coat thoroughly. Sprinkle with sesame seeds. Serve warm or store in closed container.

Open sesame!

Microwave method: In 2-cup glass measure, microwave tahini, butter, soy sauce, lemon juice, sesame oil, garlic powder and cayenne until melted. Stir. Continue as above.

Yield: 8 cups.

TAFFY POP-BALLS

8 cups popcorn   25-30 pieces taffy

Place popcorn in large greased bowl.

Melt taffy in heavy saucepan over low heat. Stir.

Dribble over popcorn and coat thoroughly.

Grease hands and form mixture into balls, using about ½ cupful for each. Serve immediately, or store covered at room temperature (taffy hardens when refrigerated).

Have an old-fashioned popcorn pull.

Microwave method: Place taffy in 3-quart glass casserole. Microwave on high until melted. Stir frequently. Continue as above.

Calorie cutter: Use sugar-free taffy.

Variations: Stir in nuts, chocolate chips, coconut, raisins, banana chips, instant coffee or other treats before forming into balls.

Yield: 14-16 popcorn balls.

GINGER SNAP CORN

8 cups popcorn
¼ cup light corn syrup
½ cup molasses
¼ cup butter

⅛ teaspoon powdered ginger
1 cup coarsely crumbled
  ginger snaps

Place popcorn in large greased bowl.

Combine corn syrup, molasses, butter and ginger in 1-quart saucepan. Bring to boil, stirring constantly. Continue without stirring to hard ball stage.*

Pour over popcorn. Stir to coat evenly. Toss crumbled ginger snaps into mixture. Cool before serving.

Ginger snap corn and I don't care.

Microwave method: Place corn syrup, molasses, butter and ginger in 2-quart glass casserole. Microwave on high 2-3 minutes until mixture reaches hard ball stage.* Stir every minute. Continue as above.

Yield: 9 cups.

*See Page 6.

BERRY PATCH

8 cups popcorn
2 tablespoons butter
¼ cup light corn syrup

¾ cup berry preserves,
  any flavor
5 drops red or blue food
  coloring, optional

Place popcorn in large greased bowl.

Combine butter, corn syrup, preserves and matching food coloring, if desired, in saucepan over low heat. Bring to boil, stirring constantly. Continue cooking for 2-3 minutes. Remove from heat.

Pour over popcorn. Stir to coat evenly. Serve as is, or place bowl in freezer for 1 hour before serving.

You'll get stuck on this!

Microwave method: Combine butter, corn syrup, preserves and food coloring in 2-quart glass casserole. Microwave on high 2-3 minutes. Stir every minute. Continue as above.

Yield: 8 cups.

POPCORN, AMERICAN-STYLE

ALASKAN SNOWBALLS

8 cups popcorn

¾ cup light corn syrup

2 tablespoons butter

⅛ teaspoon salt

¼ teaspoon vanilla

1 cup flaked coconut

Place popcorn in large greased bowl.

Combine corn syrup, butter, salt and vanilla in small saucepan over low heat. Bring to boil, stirring constantly. Continue without stirring to hard ball stage.*

Pour over popcorn. Stir to coat evenly. Cool slightly.

Grease hands with butter and form mixture into balls, using about ½ cupful for each. Place coconut in bowl. Roll popcorn balls in coconut until coated. Place on baking sheet lined with wax paper. Freeze for 1 hour.

To be eaten, not thrown!

Microwave method: Combine corn syrup, butter, salt and vanilla in 2-quart glass casserole. Microwave on high 2-3 minutes until mixture reaches hard ball stage.* Stir every minute. Continue as above.

Variations: Roll in melted white chocolate or vanilla icing instead of coconut.

Yield: 14-16 popcorn balls.

*See page 6.

ROCKY POP TRAIL MIX

8 cups popcorn
1 cup diced dried fruit
1 cup assorted unsalted nuts

1 cup chocolate or carob chips
2 teaspoons powdered sugar
1 teaspoon cinnamon

Place popcorn in large bowl.

Toss in fruit, nuts, and chocolate or carob chips. Sift sugar and cinnamon over mixture and serve.

Great for hiking outdoors or back to the TV from the kitchen.

Calorie cutter: Sprinkle with 1-2 packets sweetener in place of sugar. Use ¼ cup fruit and nuts. Skip the chips.

Shortcut: Toss 3 cups trail mix into popcorn.

Variations: Add raisins, dates, dried papaya, pineapple, apples, figs, cashews, pecans, walnuts, peanuts, almonds, sunflower seeds or other healthy items.

Yield: 11 cups.

HAWAIIAN TROPICAL TOSS

8 cups popcorn
1 tablespoon butter
1 tablespoon pineapple juice
1 cup flaked coconut
1 cup crumbled banana chips

½ cup diced dried pineapple
½ cup unsalted macadamia nuts
  or cashews
½ cup diced dried papaya
1 tablespoon powdered sugar

Place popcorn in large bowl.

Melt butter in small pan over low heat. Remove from heat. Stir in pineapple juice and coconut.

Dribble over popcorn. Toss with hands to coat thoroughly. Add remaining dried fruit and nuts. Sift powdered sugar over mixture and serve.

Aloha!

Calorie cutter: Use diet margarine and reduce added ingredients to ¼ cup each. Sprinkle with 1-2 packets sweetener in place of powdered sugar.

Shortcut: Toss 3 cups tropical trail mix into coated popcorn.

Yield: About 12 cups.

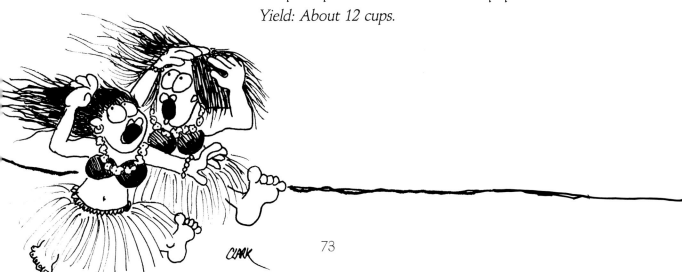

CHICAGO PAN PIZZA POP

4 cups popcorn
1 cup shredded mozzarella
cheese
1 cup shredded cheddar
cheese
1 tablespoon butter
½ cup chopped onions

¼ cup chopped mushrooms
¼ cup chopped green peppers
¼ cup sliced black olives
½ cup tomato sauce
½ teaspoon basil
½ teaspoon oregano
½ teaspoon garlic powder

Preheat oven to 375 degrees F.

Spread 2 cups popcorn in bottom of greased 8-inch round cake pan. Sprinkle with ½ cup of each cheese.

Sauté onions, mushrooms, peppers and olives in butter, in skillet, until tender. Stir in tomato sauce, basil, oregano and garlic powder. Heat thoroughly.

Spoon half of sauce over popcorn in cake pan. Top with remaining popcorn. Spread remaining sauce over top and sprinkle with remaining cheeses.

Bake for 10-12 minutes or until cheese is melted. Cut into wedges and serve.

Mama mia!!

Microwave method: Place butter in 2-quart glass casserole. Microwave on high until melted. Add onions, tomato sauce, basil, oregano and garlic powder. Microwave 1 minute on medium high. Stir. Continue as above.

Calorie cutter: Use lowfat cheeses.

Yield: 6-8 wedges.

CREOLE CRUMBLE

8 cups popcorn
1 tablespoon butter
1 tablespoon tomato paste
¼ teaspoon garlic powder
¼ teaspoon onion powder
1 teaspoon green pepper flakes
1 teaspoon celery flakes

½ teaspoon parsley flakes
1 teaspoon minced onion
¼ teaspoon black pepper
Dash cayenne pepper
⅛ teaspoon file (sassafras), optional

Place popcorn in large bowl.

Melt butter in small pan over low heat. Remove from heat. Stir in remaining ingredients.

Spoon mixture over popcorn and toss thoroughly to coat.

Eat in the French quarter or your living room, whichever is closer.

Shortcut: Substitute 1 tablespoon Creole spice mix for spices.

Yield: 8 cups.

CAJUN CORN

8 cups popcorn
2 tablespoons butter
½ teaspoon paprika
¼ teaspoon garlic powder

¼ teaspoon cayenne pepper
½ teaspoon ground white pepper
½ teaspoon ground black pepper
Bottled hot sauce, optional

Place popcorn in large bowl.

Melt butter in small pan over low heat. Remove from heat. Stir in remaining ingredients.

Dribble over popcorn and mix thoroughly to coat.

Perfect treat for just fiddling around.

Shortcut: Substitute 1 tablespoon pre-mixed Cajun spice or 1 tablespoon bottled hot sauce for spices.

Yield: 8 cups.

ARIZONA DESERT DREAM

8 cups popcorn   2 tablespoons soy sauce or tamari

Place popcorn in large bowl.
Sprinkle with soy sauce. Toss with hands to coat thoroughly.
Great with cactus juice.
Calorie cutter: Surely you jest.
Yield: 8 cups.

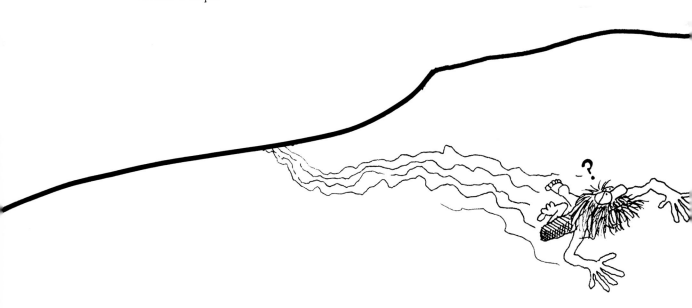

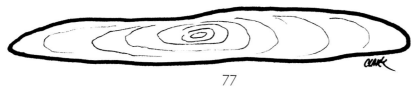

77

NASHVILLE COUNTRY POP

8 cups popcorn
1 7-ounce jar marshmallow
  cream
¼ cup melted butter
¼ cup peanut butter

2 teaspoons vanilla
1 cup flaked coconut
10 drops yellow food coloring
1 small round chocolate-
  covered cookie

Combine marshmallow cream, butter, peanut butter, vanilla, coconut and food coloring in large greased bowl.

Stir popcorn into mixture until coated evenly.

Press firmly into greased 12-inch round cake pan, forming record shape. Press cookie in center for "label." Refrigerate about 2 hours until firm. Cut into slices and serve.

Try to grab the biggest piece of this gold record – everybody else does!

Calorie cutter: Sorry, this record can't be cut.

Variations: If crunchy effect is desired, bake at 375 degrees F for 5-10 minutes. Remove and cool. Invert onto plate. It's a smash this way, too!

Yield: 1 12-inch round gold record.

TENNESSEE BAR-BE-CORN

8 cups popcorn
1 tablespoon butter
1 tablespoon tomato paste
¼ teaspoon garlic powder
¼ teaspoon onion powder

½ teaspoon brown sugar
¼ teaspoon mild vinegar
¼ teaspoon soy sauce or tamari
Cayenne pepper or hot sauce
  to taste

Place popcorn in large bowl.

Melt butter in small pan over low heat. Remove from heat. Stir in remaining ingredients.

Spoon onto popcorn. Toss with hands to coat thoroughly, and serve.

For a crunchier effect, spread popcorn mixture on greased baking sheet. Place under broiler for 1 minute. Check constantly to be sure popcorn is not burning. Remove and cool before serving.

YEE-HAH!

Shortcut: Substitute 1 tablespoon barbecue sauce for tomato paste and spices.

Variations: Add minced onions and pepper flakes.

Yield: 8 cups.

KENTUCKY FRIED KERNELS

8 cups popcorn
1 tablespoon flour
½ teaspoon salt
½ teaspoon pepper
¼ teaspoon lite lemon
  pepper
¼ teaspoon lite seasoning
  salt

1 tablespoon poultry
  seasoning
1 teaspoon paprika
1 teaspoon soy sauce or tamari
1 teaspoon water
2 tablespoons butter
1 cup cornflakes
Medium-sized paper bag

Place popcorn in large bowl.

Combine flour, salt, pepper, lemon pepper, seasoning salt, poultry seasoning and paprika in medium-sized paper bag. Shake thoroughly.

Mix soy and water and sprinkle over popcorn. Toss to dampen.

Place popcorn in bag. Shake until well-coated with flour mixture. Remove only popcorn, discarding extra flour mixture.

Melt butter in large skillet or wok. Add popcorn and cornflakes. Stir-fry until popcorn mixture becomes crispy. Remove and serve in large bucket.

The Colonel never had it so good!

Shortcut: Substitute 2 tablespoons packaged flour-type coating mix for dry ingredients in bag.

Variations: Toss in 1 tablespoon toasted sesame seeds after frying.

Yield: 9 cups.

LAS VEGAS GOLD NUGGETS

8 cups popcorn	⅛ teaspoon salt
¾ cup light corn syrup	10 drops yellow food coloring
2 tablespoons butter	1 cup toffee brickle pieces

Place popcorn in large greased bowl.

Combine corn syrup, butter, salt and food coloring in 1-quart saucepan. Bring to boil, stirring constantly. Continue without stirring to hard ball stage.* Remove from heat. Stir in toffee pieces.

Pour over popcorn. Stir to coat evenly. Cool slightly.

Grease hands and form mixture into small nugget shapes.

You can bet on this one!

Microwave method: Combine corn syrup, butter, salt and food coloring in 2-quart glass casserole. Microwave on high 2-3 minutes until mixture reaches hard ball stage.* Stir every minute. Continue as above.

Yield: About 9 cups nuggets.

*See page 6.

WISCONSIN CHEESE BALLS

8 cups popcorn
2 tablespoons butter

½ cup shredded cheese,
  any kind

Place popcorn in large bowl.

Melt butter and cheese in small pan over low heat.

Dribble over popcorn and mix thoroughly to coat. Form into balls, using about ½ cupful for each. Serve immediately or wrap and refrigerate.

If stored too long, may be used for baseballs.

Microwave method: Microwave cheese and butter until melted in 2-quart glass casserole. Continue as above.

Calorie cutter: Use lowfat cheese.
Shortcut: Use ½ cup melted processed cheese.

Variations: Add finely diced hot peppers, chopped olives, pimientos, nuts, spices or other goodies.

Yield: 10-12 popcorn balls.

HOLLYWOOD STARS

1 12-ounce package chocolate chips
1 12-ounce package butterscotch chips
½ cup peanut butter
6 cups popcorn
1 cup cornflakes
1 cup honey graham cereal
Star-shaped cookie cutter

Melt chocolate and butterscotch chips in large saucepan over low heat. Stir in peanut butter. Remove from heat. Stir in popcorn, cornflakes and cereal. Coat evenly.

Drop ¼-cup portions onto baking sheet lined with wax paper. Shape into stars with star-shaped cookie cutter. Refrigerate until firm, about 30 minutes.

An Oscar-winning treat!

Microwave method: Combine chocolate chips, butterscotch chips and peanut butter in 3-quart glass casserole. Microwave on medium high until melted. Stir every minute. Continue as above.

Calorie cutter: Jog from Hollywood to the beach before eating.

Yield: About 2 dozen.

CALIFORNIA HEALTHNUT MIX

8 cups popcorn
2 tablespoons butter
1 teaspoon soy sauce or
 tamari
¼ teaspoon garlic powder

3 tablespoons nutritional yeast
 flakes
½ cup each sunflower seeds
 and soynuts

Place popcorn in large bowl.

Melt butter in small pan over low heat. Remove from heat. Stir in soy sauce, garlic powder and 1 tablespoon yeast.

Dribble over popcorn. Toss with hands to coat thoroughly. Add seeds and nuts. Sprinkle with remaining yeast.

Eat while watching Jane Fonda videos.

Calorie cutter: No nuts – even if it IS a California recipe!

Yield: 8 cups.

NEW YORK DELI CHEESECAKE

8 cups popcorn
1 tablespoon butter
¼ teaspoon vanilla extract
1 tablespoon frozen
 lemonade, thawed

1 tablespoon instant vanilla
 pudding mix
2 tablespoons powdered sugar
1 cup crumbled graham crackers

Place popcorn in large bowl.

Melt butter in small pan over low heat. Remove from heat. Stir in vanilla, lemonade, pudding mix and 1 tablespoon powdered sugar.

Spoon onto popcorn. Toss with hands to coat thoroughly. Sprinkle remaining sugar over popcorn mixture. Toss in graham crackers. Chill before serving.

Finally, a guilt-free cheesecake – unless you don't save any for your mother!

Calorie cutter: Use diet margarine and 1 tablespoon fresh lemon juice with 2 packets sweetener in place of concentrate and sugar. Use sugar-free graham crackers or delete altogether.

Yield: 9 cups.

TEXAS CHILI TOSS

½ cup uncooked popcorn
1 tablespoon cooking oil
1 tablespoon chili oil
2 tablespoons butter
1 tablespoon tomato paste
½ teaspoon cumin
½ teaspoon chili powder
¼ teaspoon oregano

⅛ teaspoon garlic powder
⅛ teaspoon onion powder
¼ teaspoon cayenne pepper
  or to taste
2 teaspoons minced onion
2 teaspoons dried green pepper,
  optional

Pop popcorn in 1 tablespoon each cooking oil and chili oil. Set aside in large bowl.

Melt butter in small pan over low heat. Remove from heat. Stir in remaining ingredients.

Spoon mixture over popcorn. Toss with hands to coat thoroughly.

Memorize the Fire Department number beforehand.

Calorie cutter: Pop popcorn without oil.* Use diet margarine.

Shortcut: Substitute 1 tablespoon dry chili mix for tomato paste and spices.

Yield: 8 cups.

*See page 6.

FLORIDA KEY LIME KORN

8 cups popcorn
1 tablespoon butter
2 tablespoons light corn syrup
2 tablespoons limeade
  concentrate, thawed

2 tablespoons vanilla pudding
  mix
1 tablespoon powdered sugar
1 cup coarsely crumbled graham
  crackers

Place popcorn in large bowl.

Melt butter in small pan over low heat. Remove from heat. Stir in corn syrup, limeade and pudding mix.

Dribble over popcorn. Toss with hands to coat thoroughly. If mixture is too tart, dust with extra powdered sugar.

90

Spread popcorn mixture on greased baking sheet. Place under broiler for 1 minute. Check constantly to be sure popcorn is not burning. Remove and cool. Place in bowl and toss in graham crackers.

Eat while reading Hemingway.

Calorie cutter: Use 2 tablespoons fresh lime juice in place of concentrate and dust with 1-2 packets sweetener instead of sugar. Use diet margarine.

Yield: 8 cups.

GEORGIA PEACH CRUNCH

8 cups popcorn	2 tablespoons brown sugar
2 tablespoons butter	4 tablespoons peach preserves

Preheat oven to 350 degrees F.

Place popcorn in large greased bowl. Melt butter in small pan over low heat. Stir in sugar and preserves until melted.

Dribble over popcorn. Stir to coat evenly.

Spread popcorn mixture on greased baking sheet. Bake for 10 minutes. Remove and cool before serving.

Makes y'all feel right peachy!

Microwave method: Place butter in 9 x 13 x 2-inch baking dish. Microwave on high until melted. Stir in preserves and sugar. Add popcorn and stir to coat thoroughly. Microwave 3-4 minutes on high until crispy. Stir every minute.

Calorie cutter: Use diet margarine and low-cal preserves.

Yield: 8 cups.

SOUTHERN PECAN PIE POP

8 cups popcorn
¼ cup brown sugar
¾ cup maple syrup
2 tablespoons butter

⅛ teaspoon salt
¼ teaspoon maple extract
1 cup unsalted pecans

Place popcorn in large greased bowl.

Combine sugar, corn syrup, butter, salt and extract in 1-quart saucepan. Bring to boil, stirring constantly. Continue without stirring to hard ball stage.* Stir in pecans.

Pour over popcorn. Stir to coat evenly. Cool before serving.

Scarlett would trade Tara for this!

Microwave method: Combine corn syrup, butter, salt and extract in 2-quart glass casserole. Microwave on high 2-3 minutes until mixture reaches hard ball stage.* Stir every minute. Continue as above.

Yield: 9 cups.

*See page 6.

HOLIDAY POPCORN

NEW YEAR'S EVE
CHAMPAGNE POP

8 cups popcorn
2 tablespoons butter

¾ cup champagne jam
¼ cup light corn syrup

Place popcorn in large greased bowl.

Combine butter, jam and corn syrup in 1-quart saucepan over medium heat. Bring to boil, stirring constantly. Cook without stirring for 2 minutes. Remove from heat.

Pour over popcorn. Stir to coat evenly. Freeze for 1 hour and serve cold. Mixture gets sticky when warm.

Resolve to eat more popcorn this year.

Microwave method: Combine butter and jam in 2-quart glass casserole. Microwave on high 2-3 minutes. Stir every minute. Continue as above.

Yield: 8 cups.

VALENTINE HEARTS

8 cups popcorn
¼ cup red-hot candies
¾ cup light corn syrup
2 tablespoons butter

⅛ teaspoon salt
10 drops red food coloring
Heart-shaped cookie cutter

Place popcorn in large greased bowl.

Combine remaining ingredients in 1-quart saucepan over medium heat. Bring to boil, stirring constantly. Continue without stirring to hard ball stage.*

Pour over popcorn in large greased bowl. Stir to coat evenly. Cool slightly.

With greased hands, form mixture into balls, using about ½ cupful for each. Press into flat patty. Use cookie cutter or cup hands around edges to form heart shape. Cool before serving.

Aw, c'mon, have a heart!

Microwave method: Combine red-hots, corn syrup, butter, salt and food coloring in 2-quart glass casserole. Microwave on high 2-3 minutes until mixture reaches hard ball stage.* Stir every minute. Continue as above.

Yield: 14-16 hearts.

*See page 6.

GEORGE WASHINGTON CHERRY CORN

8 cups popcorn
¾ cup light corn syrup
2 tablespoons butter

½ teaspoon cherry powdered
   drink mix, unsweetened
10 drops red food coloring

Place popcorn in large greased bowl.

Combine corn syrup, butter, drink mix and food coloring in 1-quart saucepan. Bring to boil, stirring constantly. Continue without stirring to hard ball stage.*

Pour over popcorn. Stir to coat evenly. Cool slightly.

With greased hands, form into balls, using about ½ cupful for each.

It's great – I cannot tell a lie!

Microwave method: Combine corn syrup, butter, drink mix and food coloring in 2-quart glass casserole. Microwave on high 2-3 minutes until mixture reaches hard ball stage.* Stir every minute. Continue as above.

Variation: Add ¼ cup chopped maraschino cherries to popcorn before coating.

Yield: 14-16 popcorn balls.

*See page 6.

ST. PADDY'S PEPPERMINT POP

8 cups popcorn
¾ cup light corn syrup
2 tablespoons butter

½ teaspoon peppermint extract
10 drops green food coloring
Shamrock-shaped cookie cutter

Place popcorn in large greased bowl. Combine corn syrup, butter, extract and food coloring in 1-quart saucepan over medium heat. Bring to boil, stirring constantly. Continue without stirring to hard ball stage.*

Pour over popcorn. Stir to coat evenly. Cool slightly.

Grease hands. With cookie cutter, form ½-cup portions into shamrocks and place on baking sheet lined with wax paper. Cool before serving.

Erin-go-pop!

Microwave method: Combine corn syrup, butter, extract and food coloring in 2-quart glass casserole. Microwave on high 2-3 minutes until mixture reaches hard ball stage.* Stir every minute. Continue as above.

Yield: 14-16 shamrocks.

*See page 6.

MOTHER'S DAY HAM SALAD

8 cups popcorn
1 tablespoon mayonnaise
¼ teaspoon liquid or dry
smoke seasoning

½ teaspoon Worcestershire
sauce
⅛ teaspoon paprika
⅛ teaspoon cayenne pepper

Place popcorn in large bowl.

Combine mayonnaise, smoke seasoning, Worcestershire sauce, paprika and cayenne pepper.

Spoon onto popcorn. Toss with hands to coat thoroughly.

Pigs and I both love this version of one of my mom's recipes.

Yield: 8 cups.

4TH OF JULY PATRIOTIC POP

9 cups popcorn
1 cup light corn syrup
2 tablespoons butter
2 tablespoons strawberry
preserves

2 tablespoons blueberry
preserves
10 drops each red and blue
food coloring

Divide popcorn into three separate greased bowls.

Combine corn syrup and butter in 1-quart saucepan over medium heat. Bring to boil, stirring constantly. Continue without stirring to hard ball stage.*

Pour ⅓ cup corn syrup mixture over popcorn in one bowl. Stir to coat evenly.

Pour ⅓ cup corn syrup mixture into large cup or bowl. Stir in strawberry preserves and red food coloring. Pour over second bowl of popcorn. Stir to coat evenly.

Stir blueberry preserves and blue food coloring into remaining mixture in pan. Pour over third bowl of popcorn. Stir to coat evenly.

Cool, then mix together in large bowl for red, white and blue effect.

Start your 4th with a pop!

Microwave method: Combine corn syrup and butter in 2-quart glass casserole. Microwave on high 2-3 minutes until mixture reaches hard ball stage.* Stir every minute. Continue as above.

Yield: 9 cups.

*See page 6.

HALLOWEEN PUMP-KORN

8 cups popcorn
2 tablespoons butter
⅛ teaspoon ground cloves
1 teaspoon cinnamon

1 tablespoon canned pumpkin
 or pie mix
1 teaspoon brown sugar
1 tablespoon powdered sugar,
 optional

Place popcorn in large bowl.

Melt butter in small pan over low heat. Remove from heat. Stir in ground cloves, cinnamon, pumpkin and brown sugar.

Spoon onto popcorn. Toss with hands to coat thoroughly. Sprinkle with 1 tablespoon powdered sugar, if desired.

Try to save some for the trick-or-treaters.

Calorie cutter: Use diet margarine and 2 packets sweetener instead of sugar.

Yield: 8 cups.

CRANBERRY CRUMBLE

8 cups popcorn
1 tablespoon butter
1 tablespoon honey

4 tablespoons jellied
cranberry sauce

Place popcorn in large greased bowl.

Melt butter, honey and cranberry sauce in small pan over low heat. Stir thoroughly and remove from heat.

Pour over popcorn. Toss with hands to coat thoroughly. Cool before serving.

Serve with Pilgrim Pop. Your friends will think you spent the whole day cooking!

Microwave method: Place butter, honey and cranberry sauce in 2-cup glass measure. Microwave on high until melted. Continue as above.

Yield: 8 cups.

PILGRIM POP

8 cups popcorn
2 tablespoons butter
¼ teaspoon thyme
⅛ teaspoon sage
¼ teaspoon marjoram

¼ teaspoon onion powder
¼ teaspoon garlic powder
½ teaspoon chives
¼ teaspoon celery flakes

Place popcorn in large bowl.

Melt butter in small pan over low heat. Remove from heat. Stir in remaining ingredients.

Dribble over popcorn. Toss with hands to coat thoroughly.

A turkey's favorite Thanksgiving dinner.

Shortcut: Substitute 1 tablespoon poultry seasoning for spices.

Variations: Add ½ cup stuffing ingredients – diced celery, raisins, nuts, seasoned croutons or other favorites.

Yield: 9 cups.

CHRISTMAS CANDY CANE CORN

8 cups popcorn
1 cup light corn syrup
2 tablespoons butter

½ teaspoon peppermint extract
10 drops each red and green
food coloring

Divide popcorn into two large greased bowls.

Combine corn syrup, butter and extract in 1-quart saucepan over medium heat. Bring to boil, stirring constantly. Continue without stirring to hard ball stage.*

Pour ½ cup corn syrup mixture into large cup or bowl. Stir in red food coloring. Dribble red mixture over one bowl of popcorn. Stir to coat evenly. Cool.

Stir green food coloring into remaining mixture in pan. Dribble green mixture over popcorn in second bowl. Stir to coat evenly. Cool, then mix with red popcorn.

Save some for Santa.

Microwave method: Combine corn syrup, butter and extract in 2-quart glass casserole. Microwave on high 2-3 minutes until mixture reaches hard ball stage*. Stir every minute. Continue as above.

Variations: Add ½ cup crumbled candy canes or mints to popcorn before coating.

Yield: 8 cups.

*See page 6.

HOLIDAY EGGNOG

8 cups popcorn	¼ teaspoon nutmeg
2 tablespoons butter	1 tablespoon dried egg mix
2 tablespoons instant vanilla pudding mix	¼ teaspoon rum extract

Place popcorn in large bowl.

Melt butter in small pan over low heat. Remove from heat. Stir in 1 tablespoon vanilla pudding mix, nutmeg, egg mix and rum extract.

Spoon onto popcorn and toss until coated. Sprinkle with remaining pudding mix and serve.

For a crunchier effect, spread popcorn mixture onto greased baking sheet. Place under broiler for 1 minute. Check constantly to be sure popcorn is not burning. Remove and cool before serving.

Don't nog it until you've tried it!

Shortcut: Make coating mixture with melted butter and 1 tablespoon liquid eggnog.

Yield: 8 cups.

BIRTHDAY SURPRISE BALLS

8 cups popcorn
¾ cup light corn syrup
2 tablespoons butter
⅛ teaspoon salt

"Surprise" options: caramels,
taffy pieces, peanut butter cups,
chocolate or carob chips, raisins,
dates, berries or other treats

Place popcorn in large greased bowl.

Combine corn syrup, butter and salt in 1-quart saucepan over medium heat. Bring to boil, stirring constantly. Continue without stirring to hard ball stage.*

Pour over popcorn. Stir to coat evenly. Cool slightly.

With greased hands, using ½-cup portions, form mixture into balls around each treat.

You won't even mind getting older!

Microwave method: Combine corn syrup, butter and salt in 2-quart glass casserole. Microwave on high 2-3 minutes until mixture reaches hard ball stage.* Stir every minute. Continue as above.

Yield: 14-16 popcorn balls.

*See page 6.

WEDDING POPCAKE

8 cups popcorn

1 16-ounce can prepared
vanilla icing

Place popcorn in large bowl.

Melt 1 cup icing in medium saucepan over low heat.

Pour over popcorn. Stir to coat evenly.

Press into well-greased 8-inch cake pan. Refrigerate 1 hour. Turn out onto plate. Frost sides and top with remaining icing. Place miniature wedding couple on top. Make more layers for bigger weddings.

Aren't you glad he popped the question?

Calorie cutter: Hey, you're married now. Why worry about calories?

Yield: 8-10 slices.

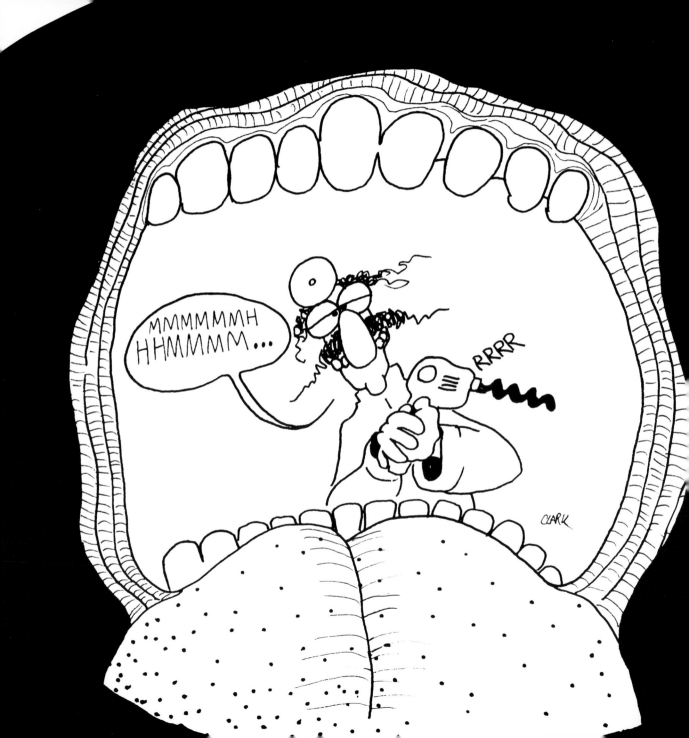

DENTISTS' DELIGHT

TOLL HOUSE POP-COOKIES

8 cups popcorn	2 tablespoons butter
¾ cup granulated sugar	⅛ teaspoon salt
¼ cup light corn syrup	1 cup chocolate chips

Place popcorn in large greased bowl.

Combine sugar, corn syrup, butter and salt in 1-quart saucepan over medium heat. Bring to boil, stirring constantly. Continue without stirring to hard ball stage.*

Pour over popcorn. Stir to coat evenly. Cool slightly.

With greased hands, form mixture into balls, using about ½ cupful for each. Flatten into very flat cookies. Cool slightly. Press chocolate chips into cookies.

Place on baking sheet lined with wax paper. Freeze for 1 hour before serving.

You'll be a pop-cookie monster after this!

Microwave method: Combine sugar, corn syrup, butter and salt in 2-quart glass casserole. Microwave on high 2-3 minutes until mixture reaches hard ball stage.* Stir every minute. Continue as above.

Variations: If crunchy cookies are desired, spread cookies on greased baking sheet and place in 375-degree F oven for 8-10 minutes. Cool before serving.

Yield: 14-16 pop-cookies.

*See page 6.

ROCKY ROAD

8 cups popcorn
1 cup chopped unsalted nuts
2 tablespoons butter

1 cup chocolate chips
1 7-ounce jar marshmallow
  cream

Combine popcorn and nuts in large greased bowl.

Melt butter and chocolate in large saucepan over low heat. Remove from heat and stir in marshmallow cream.

Dribble over popcorn mixture. Stir to coat evenly.

Press in greased 9-inch square casserole and refrigerate until firm, about 4 hours. Cut into bars and serve.

Now, remember – your mom taught you to share!

Microwave method: Place butter and chocolate in 2-quart glass casserole. Microwave on medium high, 3-4 minutes, until melted. Stir every minute. Continue as above.

Yield: About 18 bars.

118

POPWICHES

8 cups popcorn
¾ cup granulated sugar
¼ cup light corn syrup
2 tablespoons butter
⅛ teaspoon salt

Filling options: ice cream,
  frozen yogurt, peanut butter,
  marshmallow cream, preserves
1 cup melted chocolate,
  optional

Place popcorn in large greased bowl.

Combine sugar, corn syrup, butter and salt in 1-quart saucepan over medium heat. Bring to boil, stirring constantly. Continue without stirring to hard ball stage.*

Pour over popcorn. Toss with hands to coat thoroughly.

Cool slightly. With greased hands, form mixture into balls, using about ½ cupful for each.

Place on baking sheet lined with wax paper. Freeze for 5 minutes. Remove and press each ball into very flat cookie.

Spread desired filling evenly on one cookie and top with another cookie, pressing lightly. Freeze for 1 hour before serving...

. . . if you can wait that long!

Chocolate option: Coat each side of cookie with melted chocolate. Freeze for 20 minutes. Remove and spread with desired filling.

Microwave method: Combine sugar, corn syrup, butter and salt in 2-quart glass casserole. Microwave on high 2-3 minutes until mixture reaches hard ball stage.* Stir every minute. Continue as above.

Yield: 8 popwiches.

*See page 6.

DATE-NUT NIBBLE

8 cups popcorn
1 cup chopped unsalted
  walnuts or pecans
¼ cup chopped dates

1 tablespoon butter
2 tablespoons honey
4 tablespoons date pie
  filling

Toss popcorn, nuts and dates in large greased bowl.

Melt butter and honey in small pan over low heat. Remove from heat. Stir in filling.

Dribble over popcorn mixture. Stir to coat evenly.

The nuttiest date you've ever had!

Microwave method: Place butter and honey in 2-cup glass measure. Microwave on high until melted. Continue as above.

Calorie cutter: Use diet margarine and 2 tablespoons date filling. Decrease nuts to 2 tablespoons. Skip the chopped dates and honey.

Yield: About 9 cups.

CARAMEL CORN

8 cups popcorn
¾ cup brown sugar
¼ cup light corn syrup
2 tablespoons butter

⅛ teaspoon salt
½ teaspoon vanilla extract
1 cup unsalted peanuts,
  optional

Place popcorn in large greased bowl.

Combine brown sugar, corn syrup, butter and salt in 1-quart saucepan over medium heat. Bring to boil, stirring constantly. Continue without stirring to hard ball stage.* Stir in vanilla.

Pour over popcorn. Stir to coat evenly. Toss in peanuts, if desired. Cool and serve.

Hide a secret toy in the bowl, if you must.

Microwave method: Combine brown sugar, corn syrup, butter and salt in 2-quart glass casserole. Microwave on high 2-3 minutes until mixture reaches hard ball stage.* Stir every minute. Continue as above.

Shortcut: Melt 1 pound caramels with ¼ cup half-and-half. Pour over popcorn.

Yield: 8 cups.

*See page 6.

MALTED MILK BALLS

8 cups popcorn
¾ cup light corn syrup
2 tablespoons butter
⅛ teaspoon salt

3 tablespoons malted milk
  powder
2 cups chocolate chips,
  melted

Place popcorn in greased bowl.

Combine corn syrup, butter, salt and malted milk powder in 1-quart saucepan over medium heat. Bring to boil, stirring constantly. Continue without stirring to hard ball stage.*

Pour over popcorn. Stir to coat evenly. Cool slightly.

Grease hands and form mixture into balls, using about ½ cupful for each.

Place melted chocolate in bowl. Roll popcorn balls in chocolate until coated. Place on baking sheet lined with wax paper. Freeze for 1 hour before serving.

Your dentist will love this one!

Microwave method: Combine corn syrup, butter and salt in 2-quart glass casserole. Microwave on high 2-3 minutes until mixture reaches hard ball stage.* Stir every minute. Continue as above.

Yield: 14-16 popcorn balls.

*See page 6.

CHOCOLATE-COVERED CHERRY BALLS

8 cups popcorn
¾ cup cherry preserves
¼ cup light corn syrup

1 tablespoon butter
1 12-ounce package chocolate
  chips, melted

Place popcorn in large greased bowl.

Melt preserves, corn syrup and butter in saucepan over low heat. Bring to boil, stirring constantly. Continue for 3-4 minutes without stirring.

Pour over popcorn. Stir to coat evenly. Spread mixture on baking sheet lined with wax paper. Freeze for 30 minutes. Remove.

With greased hands, form mixture into balls, using about ½ cupful for each. Place chocolate in bowl.

Roll popcorn balls in chocolate until coated. Freeze for 1 hour before serving.

Life is just a bowl of chocolate-covered cherry popcorn balls.

Microwave method: Combine preserves, corn syrup and butter in 2-quart glass casserole. Microwave on high 2-3 minutes, stirring every minute. Continue as above.

Variations: Add chopped maraschino cherries to popcorn mixture before forming balls.

Yield: 14-16 popcorn balls.

CHOCOLATE MINT PATTIES

8 cups popcorn
¾ cup light corn syrup
2 tablespoons butter

½ teaspoon peppermint extract
10 drops green food coloring
2 cups melted chocolate

Place popcorn in large greased bowl.

Combine corn syrup, butter, extract and food coloring in 1-quart saucepan over medium heat.

Bring to boil, stirring constantly.

Continue without stirring to hard ball stage.* Pour over popcorn. Stir to coat evenly. Cool slightly.

Grease hands and form mixture into balls, using about ½ cupful for each. Flatten into patties. Coat each side of patty with melted chocolate. Place on baking sheet lined with wax paper. Freeze for 1 hour before serving.

My twin sister and I ate too many chocolate mint patties one Halloween and SHE still won't touch 'em – but I'm sure YOU'LL love this!

Microwave method: Combine corn syrup, butter, extract and food coloring in 2-quart glass casserole. Microwave on high 2-3 minutes until mixture reaches hard ball stage.* Stir every minute. Continue as above.

Variations: Melt chocolate mint patties in place of chocolate (groan).

Yield: 14-16 patties.

*See page 6.

MARSHMALLOW KRISPY KORN

8 cups popcorn
1 cup puffed rice cereal
3 tablespoons butter

1 7-ounce jar marshmallow
   cream

Combine popcorn and cereal in large greased bowl.

Melt butter in medium saucepan over low heat. Remove from heat. Stir in marshmallow cream.

Pour over popcorn mixture. Stir to coat evenly. Press mixture into greased 9-inch square baking pan. Refrigerate until firm, about 4 hours. Cut into bars.

Eat as one big square, if it makes you feel less guilty.

Yield: About 18 bars.

BRITTLE BREAK

8 cups popcorn	2 tablespoons molasses
1 cup roasted unsalted peanuts or almonds	2 tablespoons butter or margarine
1 cup sugar	1 teaspoon vinegar
½ cup light corn syrup	1 teaspoon baking soda

Combine popcorn and nuts in greased 9 x 13 x 2-inch baking pan.

Combine sugar, corn syrup, molasses, butter and vinegar in saucepan over low heat. Stir until sugar is dissolved. Continue without stirring over medium heat, until mixture reaches hard crack stage.* Remove from heat.

Quickly stir in baking soda and pour immediately over popcorn mixture. Stir to coat evenly.

Spread mixture onto baking sheet lined with wax paper. Cool. Break into pieces.

Go on, have a little brittle!

Microwave method: Combine sugar, corn syrup, molasses, butter and vinegar in 2-quart glass casserole. Microwave on high 5-6 minutes until mixture reaches hard crack stage.* Stir every minute. Continue as above.

Calorie cutter: Join a fitness club tomorrow.

Yield: 9 cups brittle.

*See page 6.

RUM RAISIN DELIGHT

8 cups popcorn
1 cup prepared vanilla icing
½ teaspoon rum extract

1 cup raisins
1 teaspoon cinnamon,
  optional

Place popcorn in large bowl.

Melt icing in medium saucepan over low heat. Remove from heat. Stir in extract and raisins.

Pour over popcorn. Stir to coat evenly. Sprinkle with cinnamon, if desired.

Place in greased 3-quart casserole and freeze until firm, about 30 minutes.

The perfect snack when you're raisin' cane!

Microwave method: Place icing in 2-cup glass measure. Microwave icing on high until melted. Continue as above.

Yield: 9 cups.

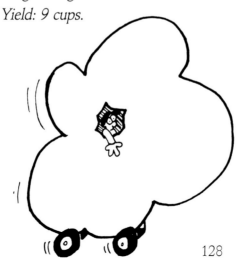

128

POP PIES

4 cups popcorn
¾ cup granulated sugar
¼ cup light corn syrup
2 tablespoons butter
¼ teaspoon salt

⅛ teaspoon cream of tartar
½ teaspoon baking soda
Filling options: pie filling,
    pudding, ice cream,
    sweetened fruit, etc.

Preheat oven to 200 degrees F.

Place popcorn in large greased bowl.

Combine sugar, corn syrup, butter, salt and cream of tartar in 1-quart saucepan over medium heat. Bring to boil, stirring constantly. Continue without stirring to hard ball stage.* Add baking soda and stir thoroughly.

Pour immediately over popcorn. Stir to coat evenly. Cool slightly.

Grease hands and press mixture into buttered 9 or 10-inch pie pan, forming shell.

Bake for 45 minutes. Cool. Fill with any variety pie filling, ice cream, pudding or other option.

Serve this elegant dessert to your upper-crust friends.

Microwave method: Combine sugar, corn syrup, butter, salt and cream of tartar in 2-quart glass casserole. Microwave on high 2-3 minutes until mixture reaches hard ball stage.* Stir every minute. Continue as above.

Variations: Make strawberry shortcake shells by pressing small amounts of popcorn mixture into greased custard dishes, forming shells. Bake at 200 degrees F for 30 minutes. Cool. Fill with sliced strawberries. Sprinkle with sugar, if desired. Top with whipped cream.

Yield: 1 pop-piecrust.

*See page 6.

POP-SICLES

8 cups popcorn
¾ cup granulated sugar
¼ cup light corn syrup
2 tablespoons butter
⅛ teaspoon salt

1 tablespoon powdered
 drink mix, or
½ teaspoon extract,
 any flavor
16 popsicle sticks
2 cups melted chocolate chips,
 optional

Place popcorn in large greased bowl.

Combine sugar, corn syrup, butter, salt and drink mix or extract in 1-quart saucepan over medium heat. Bring to boil, stirring constantly. Continue without stirring to hard ball stage.*

Pour over popcorn. Stir to coat evenly. Cool slightly.

With greased hands, scoop out about ½ cup and form an oblong shape around popsicle stick.

Place on baking sheet lined with wax paper. Freeze until firm, about 1 hour.

Big kids love 'em, too!

Chocolate option: After freezing, dip pop-sicles in melted chocolate.

Yield: 14-16 pop-sicles.

*See page 6.

DREAM POP-SICLES

8 cups popcorn
¾ cup sugar
¼ cup light corn syrup
2 tablespoons butter
2 tablespoons frozen
  orange juice, thawed

¼ teaspoon vanilla extract
1 orange rind, grated
16 popsicle sticks
1 cup prepared vanilla
  icing, melted

Place popcorn in large greased bowl.

Combine sugar, corn syrup, butter, orange juice and extracts in 1-quart saucepan over medium heat. Bring to boil, stirring constantly. Continue without stirring to hard ball stage.* Stir in rind and remove from heat.

Pour over popcorn. Stir to coat evenly. Cool slightly.

With greased hands, scoop out about ½ cup and form an oblong shape around popsicle stick.

Place on baking sheet lined with wax paper. Freeze until firm, about 1 hour.

Dip each pop-sicle in icing and return to freezer until icing hardens, about 15 minutes.

A real dream!

Microwave method: Combine sugar, corn syrup, butter, orange juice, extracts and rind in 2-quart glass casserole. Microwave on high 2-3 minutes until mixture reaches hard ball stage.* Stir every minute. Continue as above.

Yield: 14-16 pop-sicles.

*See page 6.

POP AROUND
THE CLOCK

O.J. EYE-OPENER

8 cups popcorn
¾ cup light corn syrup
2 tablespoons frozen orange
  juice concentrate
¼ teaspoon vanilla extract

¼ teaspoon orange extract,
  optional
1 tablespoon grated orange
  rind

Place popcorn in large greased bowl.

Combine corn syrup, orange juice and extracts in 1-quart saucepan. Bring to boil, stirring constantly. Continue without stirring to hard ball stage.* Stir in rind and remove from heat.

Pour over popcorn. Stir to coat evenly.

Spread popcorn mixture on greased baking sheet. Place under broiler for 1 minute. Check constantly to be sure popcorn is not burning. Remove and cool before serving.

Put a little sunshine into your popcorn.

Microwave method: Combine corn syrup, orange juice, extracts and rind in 2-quart glass casserole. Microwave on high 2-3 minutes until mixture reaches hard ball stage*. Stir every minute. Continue as above.

Yield: 8 cups.

*See page 6.

TOAST 'N JELLY POP-UP

8 cups popcorn
2 tablespoons butter
¾ cup preserves, any flavor

1 slice buttered toast,
 diced, or
1 cup toasted plain croutons

Place popcorn in large greased bowl.

Melt butter and preserves in medium saucepan over low heat. Bring to boil. Stir and remove from heat.

Pour over popcorn. Stir to coat evenly. Toss toast squares or croutons into popcorn mixture.

Place bowl in freezer for 1 hour before serving. Mixture gets sticky when warm.

I wouldn't suggest you pop THIS in your toaster.

Microwave method: Place butter and preserves in 2-cup glass measure. Microwave on high until melted. Stir every minute. Continue as above.

Yield: 9 cups.

BACORN 'N EGGS

8 cups popcorn
1 tablespoon butter
2 tablespoons powdered egg
  substitute
1 tablespoon liquid or dry
  smoke seasoning
¼ teaspoon black pepper
2 tablespoons soy bacon bits

Place popcorn in large greased bowl.

Melt butter in small pan over low heat. Remove from heat. Stir in egg mix, smoke seasoning, pepper and bacon bits.

Spoon onto popcorn. Toss with hands to coat thoroughly.

Spread popcorn mixture on greased baking sheet. Place under broiler for 1 minute. Check constantly to be sure popcorn is not burning. Remove and cool before serving.

Treat that special person to breakfast popcorn in bed.

Yield: 8 cups.

POP CRISPIES

16 cups popcorn
¼ cup light brown sugar
1 tablespoon cooking oil

1 tablespoon water
½ teaspoon vanilla
⅛ teaspoon cinnamon

Preheat oven to 300 degrees F.

Place popcorn in large bowl or roasting pan.

Mix sugar, oil, water, vanilla and cinnamon in small bowl.

Dribble over popcorn. Toss with hands to coat thoroughly.

Spread on a large greased baking sheet. Bake for 15 minutes or to desired crispness. Serve plain or with milk.

Snap... Crackle... POP!

Calorie cutter: Use 2 packets sweetener in place of sugar.

Yield: 16 cups.

CHEESE POPLET

8 cups popcorn
1 tablespoon butter
1 tablespoon powdered egg
  substitute

1 tablespoon water
¼ teaspoon salt
¼ teaspoon pepper
¼ cup shredded cheddar cheese

Place popcorn in large bowl.

Melt butter in small pan over low heat. Remove from heat. Stir in egg mix, water, salt and pepper.

Dribble onto popcorn. Toss with hands to coat thoroughly.

Spread popcorn mixture on greased baking sheet. Sprinkle with cheese.

Place under broiler for 1 minute. Check constantly to be sure popcorn is not burning. Remove and cool before serving.

Eggs-actly what you were hungry for!

Calorie cutter: Use lowfat cheese.

Variations: Add other omelet items such as soy bacon bits, minced onion, green pepper flakes, chopped mushrooms or other favorites.

Yield: 8 cups.

POPCAKES

8 cups popcorn
½ cup brown sugar
1-2 cups maple syrup

¼ cup butter
¼ teaspoon maple extract

Place popcorn in large greased bowl.

Combine brown sugar, ½ cup maple syrup, butter and extract in 1-quart saucepan. Bring to boil, stirring constantly. Continue without stirring to hard ball stage.*

Pour over popcorn. Stir to coat evenly. Cool slightly.

Grease hands and form ½-cup portions into pancake-sized patties. Pour extra maple syrup over popcakes.

You'll flip over these.

Microwave method: Combine brown sugar, maple syrup, butter and extract in 2-quart glass casserole. Microwave on high 2-3 minutes until mixture reaches hard ball stage.* Stir every minute. Continue as above.

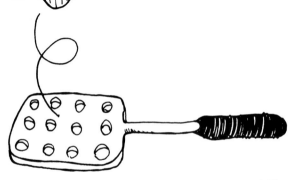

Yield: 14-16 popcakes.

*See page 6.

POP GOES GRANOLA

4 cups popcorn
2 cups quick-cooking oats
½ cup toasted shredded
  coconut
½ cup wheat germ
¼ cup butter
½ cup honey

¼ cup light brown sugar
2 teaspoons cinnamon
1 cup raisins
½ cup toasted almonds
½ cup sunflower seeds
1 tablespoon powdered sugar

Preheat oven to 300 degrees F.

Combine popcorn, oats, coconut and wheat germ in 13 x 9 x 2-inch baking dish.

Melt butter in small pan over low heat. Stir in honey, sugar and cinnamon. Remove from heat.

Dribble over popcorn mixture. Toss to coat thoroughly.

Bake for 30 minutes, stirring every 10 minutes. Toss in raisins, almonds and seeds. Sprinkle with powdered sugar and bake for 10 more minutes. Cool before serving.

Great gift for friends who like to hike and do other silly things like that.

Microwave method: Place butter in 13 x 9 x 2-inch glass baking dish. Microwave on high until melted. Stir in honey, sugar, cinnamon, oats, coconut and almonds. Microwave on high 3 minutes, stirring every minute. Toss in popcorn. Microwave on high until crisp, 1-2 minutes, stirring every minute. Remove. Stir in raisins and sunflower seeds.

Variations: Add dates, figs, dried apples, coconut, pineapples, papayas, apricots, cashews, peanuts, walnuts, pecans or other fun ingredients.

Yield: About 10 cups.

REUBEN SANDWICH

8 cups popcorn
2 tablespoons butter
½ teaspoon liquid or dry
  smoke seasoning
½ teaspoon soy sauce or
  tamari

1 tablespoon sauerkraut juice
2 tablespoons shredded
  Swiss cheese

Place popcorn in large bowl.

Melt butter in small pan over low heat. Remove from heat. Stir in smoke seasoning, soy sauce and sauerkraut juice.

Dribble over popcorn. Toss with hands to coat thoroughly.

Spread popcorn mixture on greased baking sheet and sprinkle with shredded cheese. Place under broiler for 1 minute. Check constantly to be sure popcorn is not burning. Remove and cool before serving.

I'm still trying to convince my mom to try this one!

Calorie cutter: Use diet margarine and lowfat cheese.

Yield: 8 cups.

HAM ON RYE

8 cups popcorn
2 slices toasted rye bread, cubed
1 tablespoon mayonnaise
2 teaspoons liquid or dry smoke seasoning
¼ teaspoon soy sauce or tamari
¼ teaspoon garlic powder
1 tablespoon caraway seeds, crushed

Place popcorn and rye bread cubes in large bowl.

Combine mayonnaise, smoke seasoning, soy sauce, garlic powder and caraway seeds.

Spoon onto popcorn mixture. Toss with hands to coat thoroughly.

Surprise your friends when they trade their lunch for your ham on rye!

Calorie cutter: Use diet mayonnaise and skip the bread.

Yield: About 10 cups.

POP DOG

8 cups popcorn
1 tablespoon prepared mustard
1 tablespoon mayonnaise
1 teaspoon liquid or dry smoke seasoning

Place popcorn in large bowl.

Combine mustard, mayonnaise and smoke seasoning. Spoon over popcorn. Toss with hands to coat thoroughly.

Take to the ballgame and sell the vendor some!

Yield: 8 cups.

GARDEN VEGETA-BOWL

8 cups popcorn
1½ tablespoons mayonnaise
⅛ teaspoon lite lemon pepper
¼ teaspoon dry tomato
  soup mix
⅛ teaspoon garlic powder
⅛ teaspoon onion powder

¼ teaspoon paprika
1 teaspoon dried vegetable
  flakes
½ teaspoon dried green
  pepper flakes
¼ teaspoon celery flakes

Place popcorn in large bowl.

Combine remaining ingredients in small bowl.

Dribble over popcorn. Toss with hands to coat thoroughly.

You won't have to be told to eat your vegetables!

Shortcut: Make coating mixture with 3 teaspoons dry vegetable soup mix (without noodles) and mayonnaise.

Yield: 8 cups.

P.B.J. POP

8 cups popcorn
½ cup preserves
3 tablespoons peanut butter
1 tablespoon butter

Place popcorn in large greased bowl.

Melt preserves, peanut butter and butter in small pan over low heat. Stir until smooth. Remove from heat.

Pour over popcorn. Stir to coat evenly. Place mixture in freezer for 1 hour before serving. Mixture gets sticky when warm.

Really sticks to your ribs (and the roof of your mouth and your teeth and your fingers...)

Microwave method: Place preserves, peanut butter and butter in 2-cup glass measure. Microwave on high until melted. Stir. Continue as above.

Calorie cutter: Use ¼ cup low-cal preserves, 1 tablespoon peanut butter and diet margarine.

Variations: Use 1 tablespoon mashed ripe banana or honey instead of preserves.

Yield: 8 cups.

McBACON CHEESE POP

8 cups popcorn
2 tablespoons butter
1 teaspoon liquid or dry
  smoke seasoning
1 teaspoon soy sauce or
  tamari

2-3 tablespoons shredded
  cheddar or Swiss cheese
2 tablespoons soy bacon bits

Place popcorn in large bowl.

Melt butter in small pan over low heat. Remove from heat. Stir in smoke seasoning and soy sauce.

Dribble over popcorn. Toss with hands to coat thoroughly.

Spread popcorn mixture on greased baking sheet. Sprinkle cheese and bacon bits on top. Place under broiler for 1 minute. Check constantly to be sure popcorn is not burning. Remove and cool before serving.

Is that for here or to go?

Calorie cutter: Use diet margarine and lowfat cheese.

Yield: 8 cups.

PORTERHOUSE POP

8 cups popcorn
2 tablespoons butter
1 teaspoon dry or liquid
 smoke seasoning

1 teaspoon soy sauce or
 tamari
¼ teaspoon dry onion
 bouillon

Place popcorn in large bowl.

Melt butter in small pan over low heat. Remove from heat. Stir in smoke seasoning, soy sauce and bouillon.

Dribble over popcorn. Toss with hands to coat thoroughly.

If you like yours well-done, spread popcorn mixture on greased baking sheet. Place under broiler for 1 minute. Check constantly to be sure popcorn is not burning. Remove and cool before serving.

Personally, I prefer my popcorn rare.

Yield: 8 cups.

POPCORN AU GRATIN

8 cups popcorn
2 tablespoons butter
2 tablespoons dry instant
 potato flakes

1 tablespoon dry cheese
 soup mix

Place popcorn in large bowl.

Melt butter in small pan over low heat. Remove from heat.

Dribble over popcorn. Toss with hands to coat thoroughly.

Combine potato flakes and cheese soup mix in small bowl. Sprinkle mixture over popcorn and toss again.

Serve instead of potatoes at dinner – well, maybe not on the night the boss is coming.

Variations: Substitute ¼ cup melted cheese for dry cheese soup mix.

Yield: 8 cups.

FETTU-CORN-E ALFREDO

8 cups popcorn
1 tablespoon butter
1 tablespoon smooth cottage
  cheese or plain yogurt
2 tablespoons grated
  Parmesan cheese

¼ teaspoon garlic powder
Dash nutmeg
Salt and pepper to taste

Place popcorn in large bowl.

Melt butter in small pan over low heat. Remove from heat. Stir in cottage cheese or yogurt, Parmesan cheese, garlic powder, nutmeg, salt and pepper.

Pour over popcorn. Toss with hands to coat thoroughly.

Spread popcorn mixture on greased baking sheet. Place under broiler 1 minute. Check constantly to be sure popcorn is not burning. Remove and cool before serving. Sprinkle with extra Parmesan cheese, if desired.

Bonissimo!

Calorie cutter: Use lowfat cottage cheese or yogurt. Use diet margarine and 1 tablespoon Parmesan cheese.

Yield: 8 cups.

AMARETTO TOASTED ALMOND

8 cups popcorn
½ cup toasted slivered
 almonds
¾ cup granulated sugar
¼ cup light corn syrup
2 tablespoons butter

⅛ teaspoon salt
1 teaspoon almond extract
1 tablespoon Amaretto
5 drops each red and yellow
 food coloring

Combine popcorn and almonds in large greased bowl.

Combine remaining ingredients in 1-quart saucepan. Bring to boil, stirring constantly. Continue without stirring to hard ball stage.*

Pour over popcorn mixture and coat evenly.

Check I.D.'s before serving.

Microwave method: Combine sugar, corn syrup, butter, salt, extract, Amaretto and food coloring in 2-quart glass casserole. Microwave on high 2-3 minutes until mixture reaches hard ball stage.* Stir every minute. Continue as above.

Yield: 8 cups.

*See page 6.

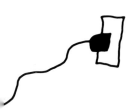

KNOW ANOTHER POPCORN LOVER?

Additional copies of:

FOR POPCORN LOVERS ONLY Cookbook $9.95/book

POPCORN LOVER'S GOURMET SEASONINGS .... $8.95/set of 3
3 oz. each taco, pizza and cajun flavors

POPCORN LOVER'S
MICROWAVE POPCORN EARS .... $2.95/set of 3
Pops right on the ear in its own special bag

Please add $1.00 shipping plus $.50 for each additional item.

Send check or money order to:
Strawberry Patch, P.O. Box 52404-P, Atlanta, GA 30355-0404.

Charge orders call 1-800-875-7242, 9am-5pm EST. VISA/MC accepted.